INVESTING FOR SELF-EMPLOYED BALLERS

WHAT TO DO WITH AND WITHOUT A 401(k)

DREW WYNN

COPYRIGHT © 2020 DREW WYNN

All rights reserved.

No part of this book may be reproduced, distributed, or transmitted without written permission from the author.

FinanceBro.net

ISBN: 979-8642068687

*For mom, dad, my brother Tuan, and Ki.
Thank you for believing in me.*

*Additional thanks to my good friends Jordan and Steve
for helping me learn the trading business.*

DISCLAIMER

The information contained in this book **SHOULD NOT be considered financial advice**. Nor should it be a substitute for financial advice from a professional, licensed or otherwise, who knows the details of your situation.

I've made best efforts to ensure that the information provided in this book is accurate, valuable, and actionable. I like to think that I really know what I'm talking about, but there's always the possibility that I don't. As such, the onus is on you to **do your own research** and due diligence before making any investment decision.

Any specific numbers (interest rates, contribution limits, etc.) were correct when this book was written in 2020. But they may have changed by the time you read it.

Investing always involves risk, and I **WILL NOT be held liable** if you lose money or sustain other losses. Use the information in this book **at your own risk**, obviously.

CONTENTS

Introduction 1

Chapter 1: How to Save 7

Chapter 2: Basic Plan 37

Chapter 3: Intermediate Concepts 55

Chapter 4: Intermediate Plans 81

Chapter 5: Advanced Concepts 93

Chapter 6: Advanced Plans 111

Chapter 7: Additional Topics 125

Conclusion 139

INTRODUCTION

There's no one more boring in this world than someone who always has money on his mind. For six years I've been trying to come up with an interesting response to "What do you do?" And for six years that conversation has fallen flat every time. What idiot would spend years of his life decoding the complex financial system just so he could manage a few pro bono accounts from his parents' basement? Well, that idiot would be me.

Even though poker's not a full-time endeavor anymore, I just lead as a "professional poker player" now. On the surface, the idea of a high-stakes gambler is way more exciting than a trader or investor who works from home. People's eyes light up when it comes to the possibility of easy money, and there's a visceral attraction to James Dean–like rebels who pursue the American Dream.

I spent most of my life chasing and eventually mastering money. Was it worth it? I probably would've made some better choices. You don't need to spend more than 15 minutes per year thinking about money though. Do anything else with your time!

White-collar professionals are America's new poor. Working 40–60 hours per week, you feel like you're stuck in the struggling upper middle class and might have to work forever. The stock market is soaring to new highs and appears to be making everyone else wealthy. You know that you should get more involved and also do something with your old 401(k). But you're too busy with your career, your business, and your family.

Let's say you make $100,000 per year and set aside $25,000 for retirement. That might be adequate compensation for your hard work, but now you have to worry about how to invest. Defined contribution plans, asset allocation, portfolios, expense ratios, prospectuses, dividends, capital gains—it all sounds like a total mess! Where do you start if you don't have a fancy MBA or CFA credential, and how do you find the courage to take that first step without feeling like the markets will run you over? Are you even allowed to manage your own money without professional qualifications? Perhaps you've opened a trading account and failed miserably.

Investing can be overwhelming for most people, and it's no surprise that hard-working professionals are willing to pay financial advisors 1–2% ($1,000–2,000 per $100,000) per year in direct management fees and another 1–3%

($1,000–3,000 per $100,000) in hidden fees. Most advisors, who are just salesmen, like to funnel your money into expensive mutual funds because they receive kickback compensation that's sometimes illegal. They also dump your money into a mix of assets that's random and thoughtless. After adding their fees up, if you're supposed to make an average of 5–6% per year in the stock market (assumptions of 10–12% are grossly incorrect), advisors will take most of your profits!

If the stock market is so intimidating that you keep a lot of money in brick-and-mortar bank accounts, know that big banks are hustling you too. Perhaps they've enticed you with tier reward programs where you move up the ranks from peasant to elite to super elite as you deposit large sums of money with them. But compare their interest rate of 0.1% to a fair money market rate that's often 1–2% higher. On a $100,000 balance, that's a $1,000–2,000 annual membership fee to pretend you're a VIP (you're not on anyone's radar until you have $10 million).

The financial industry rarely acts in their clients' best interests. When making decisions, they rarely ask, "Is this right or wrong?" They instead ask, "Is this legal or illegal, and how far can I push that line and still get away with it?" In other words, this industry is full of manipulative psychopaths who treat money like a zero-sum game, and they don't care if their actions hurt you. There's an air of distrust in the stock market, and banks, insurance companies, and other insiders keep it maximally complicated to protect their turf.

So how do you navigate your way past the vultures and swindlers with the confidence that you'll come out ahead? Is it even possible to escape the daily grind and start building real wealth? It seems so utterly hopeless, and I don't blame you for feeling disenchanted.

Through the rest of these pages, I'd like to take the weight off your shoulders and make investing easier for you. I'll walk you through the entire process step-by-step, from right this moment until you've retired with millions. You'll learn how to derive the most value from financial markets at the lowest cost. You'll effortlessly outperform 99% of all investors. And your friends and family will eventually come to YOU for investment advice!

In the spring of 2014, my parents were confused because their managed account with J.P. Morgan had earned little to nothing for years while the stock market was at all-time highs. This isn't atypical, and many others share this same concern. When you burn your hand on a hot stove, you know not to touch it again. But when you give money to a financial advisor, you don't know that you're getting burned because they cook you slowly. Your complacency allows them to skin you and bleed you.

I dissected their financial statements and realized that layers of excessive fees and poor asset allocation were to blame for drastic underperformance. Believing my fancy degree in finance counts for something, my brother asked me to solve their problem. And so I dropped my failing day-trading venture and worked diligently to build a career in long-term investing.

Despite MANY painful mistakes over the first six years, we've made a lot of money, and you certainly can too. You'll no longer be a struggling sheep like every other American, and you'll be able to work less and retire early if you want. But before you get too excited, you must first learn how to save.

1 | HOW TO SAVE

It doesn't matter if you make $300,000 per year or $30,000. This book was written with high-income professionals in mind, but it's appropriate for everyone because all that matters is how much you save. Money is a mindset, and a high income doesn't help you get your first $1–2 million.

If you have less than $100,000 and you're not saving at least $1,000 per month, you don't need investment advice. You need to create good money habits first.

MONEY MINDFULNESS

Your relationship with money and your rate of savings determine your wealth. Your income and your market return (after fees) are also important, but only after you build good habits when it comes to money.

Sometimes income doesn't matter at all. No matter how much you make, you'll always find ways to spend it. Look at the long list of celebrities who have gone broke because they never learned how to save. They splurged on

Gulfstream jets, private yachts, oceanfront mansions, and more.

Conservative financial advice tells you to start early—as early as your twenties—and makes you feel guilty for being late to the party. It's accompanied by some arbitrary calculation: If you start at the age of 25, $1,000 per month growing at 12% per year is $9 million by the time you're 65. But if you wait until 35, you'll only have $3 million. Look at the $6 million you missed out on!

This reminds me of when I volunteered at a support group for recovering alcoholics. At one particular meeting, I was feeling bad about myself for drinking too much the night before and hooking up with a relatively unattractive girl. When I shared this with the group, the facilitator prompted everyone, "Raise your hand if you've ever done this." Every hand in the room went up.

So don't feel guilty if you're 30 or 40 years old and still don't know how to save. You are not alone if you have less than $100,000! We need at least 10 years as adults to pay down debt and get all the dumb spending out of our system. It takes time to develop *some* maturity around money.

You can be mindful of how you spend without being cheap. I'm not telling you to make big sacrifices, skip your $5 latte every morning, or spend your life denying yourself small pleasures. Just pay attention to where spending might be unnecessary—the next section is full of hidden gems.

Many people listen to money podcasts, follow arbitrary heuristics, and detail every penny spent in various budgeting apps. The "personal finance" genre is a total joke. You don't need a calorie-counting app and personal trainers to lose weight—you just need to sleep more and cut grains, sugar, and other junk from your diet. And if you never buy these foods at the grocery store, you never have to fight the temptation to eat carb-laden peasant food at home.

Guess what? Money works like this too. You can easily accumulate $1–2 million without worrying about how to generate a bigger income, how to start your own business, or how to get involved in real estate. All you have to do is save 25–50% of your income (before taxes). It's challenging, and you might feel like you don't make enough to be able to do that. But if you don't start TODAY, you'll ALWAYS find an excuse to never have enough to start.

BREAKING IT DOWN

"It's TOO HARD!" That's the argument I hear all the time, and it doesn't matter if they're making $30,000 per year or $100,000. Nobody likes to hear this—if you keep telling yourself, "It's TOO HARD," you'll believe that it's true and won't do anything about it.

Life is tough—I get it. The last thing you want to think about is how to be happy with less. Let's break it down right now and find you $1,000 per month ($12,000 per year) to save.

It took me a while to mature. I was making over $100,000 per year right out of college, but my total savings was stuck at $100,000 for a decade. I spent money on dumb things like a $50,000 sports car, a personal chef, and two-bedroom apartments in the most expensive neighborhoods of big cities. It wasn't until I moved back into my parents' basement for a few years that I developed better habits around money. Hopefully you won't make the same mistakes.

HOUSING

If you're self-employed and live on your own, you don't need a second bedroom as a guest room, home office, or "safe space" for fragile little snowflakes. Any bedroom that's not being slept in year-round is a huge waste of money. I'm a fancy trader who uses lots of monitors and desk space, and yet my "home office" is only a six-foot by six-foot section of my living room.

My family visits me once per year (maybe your family loves you more and visits you more often), and instead of spending an extra **$200+ per month ($2,400+ per year)** on a second bedroom, they can stay in a nice Airbnb or hotel for a week (use Priceline Express Deals to save **$500+ per year** on hotels). Whether you rent or own, do not pay for a home with more bedrooms than you need to sleep in.

Some people are anal like me and need their own quiet nest. But if you can lean into small discomforts, you'll save another **$400+ per month ($4,800+ per year)** by living with a compatible roommate.

If you're a real estate agent, you might be paying **$500–1,200 per month ($6,000–14,400 per year)** for a private office that's seldom needed. Freelancers can work from home and meet their 15 clients per year in a coworking space, a coffee shop, or their apartment community's clubhouse.

If you want to buy a home, plan on living there for at least 7–10 years to recoup transaction costs. Also understand that properties listed on broker websites tend to overstate a home's true value by 20–30%. Negotiate directly with sellers if possible. And if a scummy realtor with a 7% fee won't respond to your bid (or "offer") unless it's within $10,000 of her listing price, call her on her bluff and move on to other properties.

For a $245,000 listing, $173,500 is a good bid to start with. Initiate a conversation and feel out the seller. If she's being stubborn, throw in a second bid of $193,900. Don't be eager to please her—see how low she's willing to go. When she's firm in her final offer, pray that it's below your maximum bid of $204,200. If it isn't, move on to other properties.

Effective negotiation is about understanding your options, especially the less obvious ones, and being willing to walk away from every offer until you get what you want. You reframe the world to fit your vision. Whose reality is stronger—yours or hers? Real estate agents know deep down that their job isn't real and their commissions aren't sustainable. They NEED the money, and they're desperate to close the deal. If you're not equally desperate to buy a home because you know your options, your reality wins.

Also, ignore any notion of a "fair" price. In any marketplace, the original cost of a particular good is always irrelevant. Prices fluctuate every day, and the only valid price is the highest bid at that time. Unless you're buying a Fabergé egg, there's always a substitute for everything. Be patient, and never set your heart on any single home no matter how nice it is.

Don't ever let anyone rush you into making a decision either. Salesmen know you'll make mistakes if they force an arbitrary deadline on you, so walk away if they're too aggressive! You'll buy and sell a few homes in your lifetime, and you can save **$1,000–5,000 per year** with basic negotiation skills.

Go to a credit union for your mortgage because the best ones have an interest rate that's lower than banks. A 0.5% difference on a $200,000 mortgage can save you **$50 per month ($600 per year)**. This may not seem like much, but 10 of these quick wins nets you $500 per month ($6,000 per year) in free money (little things count!). Find these hidden gems in your life and fight for every dollar!

TRANSPORTATION

If you live in a major city, you probably don't need a car. I lived in Chicago and worked 60–80 hours per week from home, and yet I spent **$250 per month ($3,000 per year)** on parking to use my car just a few times each month! I should've sold my car and used public transportation, Uber, and Zipcar to save **$500+ per month ($6,000+ per year)** in car payments, insurance, registration fees, maintenance, gas, and tolls.

America is the land of big. We like our pickup trucks and SUVs, and it's our American right to take up space and pollute the world!

You don't need a big car unless you're trying to signal higher status with meaningless consumer symbols of identity. Save money by taking a defensive driving course, buying a mid-size sedan with understated style like a Volkswagen Passat, and equipping it with seasonally appropriate tires (you don't need AWD to drive effectively through snow). Your suburban kids will be just as safe coming home from soccer practice. And you can fit four snowboards on a car rack for your annual trip to Aspen.

Salesmen hustled me twice for new cars because I went into their dealerships eager and unprepared. Look up actual transaction prices on TrueCar.com. Just like realtors, car dealers have thousands of dollars to negotiate with, so be patient and walk away from every offer until you get what you want. You'll always get hustled a little bit whenever you make a transaction with a dealer. I made two transactions in one visit when I traded in my car for another one, and they screwed me over.

You could try private transactions, but there are lots of cars with unreported accidents and hidden damage. Low mileage doesn't guarantee higher quality either.

If you follow the recommended maintenance schedule (use an independent mechanic, never dealerships unless it's for free warranty work), you can drive each car for 200,000–300,000 miles. This would minimize the number of transactions in your lifetime. Hopefully you're not a disgusting redneck who throws away Burger King wrappers on the floor. I keep my car (and everything else I own) clean, and people still think a 2013 Ford Fusion with 150,000 miles is brand new!

God forbid you make the huge mistake of leasing a car. Don't use financing at the dealership either. The rates they offer are egregious, and even with a 0% deal, they're still getting the better of you with a higher car price.

Banks are terrible too—they charge interest of over 3% per year plus application fees. Call different credit unions for the lowest rate (1–1.5% right now), and get pre-approved for a loan before you start shopping.

Let's say you're a typical upper-middle-class American who buys a big pickup truck or SUV for $34,000 ($1,000 less than the $35,000 MSRP) and trades it in for $7,000 every 7 years. You pay $2,000 for extended warranty and other unnecessary add-ons and get a 3% interest loan from a bank. Your payment is about $400 per month.

Now let's say you're a savvy saver who buys a mid-size sedan for $22,000 (or $3,000 less than the $25,000 MSRP). You get a 1.5% interest loan from a credit union, keep your car clean and well-maintained, and donate it to a younger relative in 14 years. Your payment is now about $300 per month for the first 7 years and nothing for the next 7 years—$150 per month on average. This is **$250 per month ($3,000 per year)** you're saving on payments, and you'll save another $30 per month **($360 per year)** on gas!

HEALTH INSURANCE

I use Obamacare because my income is less than $50,000 per year before deferred investment gains. It's great, so definitely take advantage of its **$6,000 per year** benefit if you qualify. You might also consider Obamacare if you're self-employed and have variable income that's under $50,000 in some years.

Choose a Silver plan because it offers substantial savings over Bronze and Gold. Don't pay the **$30 per month ($360 per year)** for dental. You can get cleanings for $25 and x-rays for $35 at the dental clinic of a local college.

You're probably healthy if you sleep 7–8 hours every night, you avoid grains and sugar, you exercise, you spend time outdoors in direct sunlight, and you try not to multi-task. If you can't get any subsidies, you might be better off without health insurance. This applies to other types of insurance where you're a lower risk too.

If you're not a jittery cokehead who frequently leaves the stove burner on, don't get home insurance. If you're not a bad parent with a violent child or pit bull, don't get liability insurance. If you're not an aggressive driver like me, get the minimum auto insurance required by law (I max out liability and remove everything else—I pay only $30 per month). Insurance is a game where most people lose, so don't participate unless you take the time to understand that game.

GROCERIES AND SUPPLIES

My friend Amelia once said, "Eating healthy is expensive. But you know what's more expensive? Cancer." I totally agree, and I don't skimp on food when it can improve my quality of life. You don't have to be ridiculous like me—lots of red meat and everything organic, grass-fed, pasture-raised, etc. But you don't need to eat out every day (it's impossible to be healthy if you do).

I spend $10,000 per year on groceries, which is probably excessive. But I save **$5,000 per year** because I buy in bulk, meal prep each week, and eat the same delicious meals every day. The Amazon Prime credit card gives me a 5% discount (sometimes more) on all of my shopping at Whole Foods and on Amazon. When groceries and supplies are on sale—$1 off local eggs, 50¢ off Siggi's Icelandic yogurt (plus the 10% case discount), $3 off LaCroix sparkling water, $11 off Harbison cheese, $1 off Kerrygold Irish butter—I'll stock up for months. People think I'm crazy when I buy 20 tubs of butter, but then I look at the Doritos in their cart with equal disdain. The meat department guys know me by name, and if I ask, they'll often give me a 15% discount on my 10-pound weekly order of meat and maybe free bone marrow too.

Anyone can eat a healthy diet of chicken quarters (let other people pay double for dry, boneless, skinless breast), vegetables, eggs, Greek yogurt, and cheese for well under $5,000 per year. Amazon's Subscribe & Save program will save you a lot of money on supplies too.

COFFEE

Again, I'm not telling you to deny yourself a $5 coffee every morning if it makes you happy. But if you're rushing to a dead-end corporate job, I promise you're not getting its full value. If you're going to spend $5 on coffee, go into the coffee shop, tip the barista $1, and sit down. Turn off your smartphone and laptop, and take 15 minutes for yourself.

You could also make coffee on your own. For two weeks' worth of the best cold brew coffee you will ever have, buy a Toddy filtration system on Amazon, grind fresh Komodo Dragon Blend whole beans from Starbucks, brew for 12–24 hours, and then let it drip into the decanter.

Pour over ice with some condensed milk and evaporated milk when you want to drink it.

Bone broth is my guilty pleasure, and I used to spend $100 per month for a commercialized version of this delicacy. For three weeks' worth of savory bone broth, save all your beef and chicken bones until they fill a grocery bag (nothing goes to waste!), throw the bones in a 12-quart stockpot, add some aromatics (onion, garlic, celery, carrots, salt, pepper, bay leaves), top off with water, simmer for 48 hours, and then pour it through a strainer into wide-mouth mason jars. Whether you drink coffee or bone broth every day, you'll save **$1,000–2,000 per year** making it yourself!

CREDIT CARDS

Most people shouldn't use credit cards. The average balance is almost $10,000 per household, and at 20% interest, that's **$2,000 per year** you're pissing away. If you don't pay your balances in full every month, pull out all of your credit cards and cancel them right now. Pay down any residual balances as soon as possible and never apply for another one again!

Credit is a game that rewards wealthy financiers for preying on everyone else. Only people with *exceptional* financial discipline can beat them. This game is measured by a credit score, which isn't as important as everyone thinks it is. If you live beyond your means and need expensive loans to acquire meaningless consumer symbols of identity, you should just pay cash for everything. This will prevent you from falling into a credit trap that ends with bankruptcy.

In the 15 years that I've had credit cards, I've always paid them off in full every month. This might be because of my OCD, but I'm rewarded with **$1,000+ per year** in cashback and a perfect 850 FICO score. If you set up automatic payments in full from your bank account every month, here are a few credit cards you can use for maximum cashback—

- *Amazon Prime Rewards*
  Earn 5% at Whole Foods and on Amazon; 2% at restaurants, gas stations, and drugstores; and 1% on everything else. Plus a $70 Amazon gift card. Requires an Amazon Prime membership.

- *American Express Blue Cash Preferred*

  Earn 6% at supermarkets and on streaming TV; 3% on transit (Uber, parking, tolls, trains, buses, etc.) and gas; and 1% on everything else. Plus a $250 bonus if you spend $1,000 in the first three months. $95 annual fee.

- *Uber*

  Earn 5% on Uber; 3% on restaurants and travel; and 1% on everything else. Plus a $100 bonus if you spend $500 in the first three months.

- *Costco Anywhere*

  Earn 4% on gas; 3% on restaurants and travel; 2% at Costco; and 1% on everything else. Requires a Costco membership.

- *U.S. Bank Cash+*

  Don't carry more than three credit cards around because you won't remember where to use each one. Just link this one to your automatic payments for utilities, cell phones, cable internet, streaming TV, and gym memberships to earn 5%. Plus a $150 bonus if you spend $500 in the first three months.

- *Fidelity Rewards*

    Earn 2% on everything. You can deposit your rewards directly into your Fidelity Brokerage Account that you'll soon open!

BANK BONUSES

Go to DoctorOfCredit.com, and under the Bank Accounts menu, click Best Bank Account Bonuses for the current month. You'll see a list of available bonuses that you can milk from different banks. You'll need direct deposits into these accounts to clear a few of the bonuses, but this can usually be done by transferring money out of and back into your Fidelity Brokerage Account. It's a little bit of work to capture each bonus, but you can pick up **$3,000 per year** in free money.

HEAT AND A/C

I won't harp on you too much here—most people are pretty good (cheap even) about regulating heat, air conditioning, and other energy usage. When I first moved to the South, I had no idea what a heat pump was and left my thermostat in HEAT mode. Not only was the heating unit running every minute of the day, but cold air was being pushed into my apartment too. My electricity bill was $200–300 per month that first winter!

I have no idea why southern heating systems are designed this way, but I use the more energy-efficient EMERGENCY mode now. In the winter, I keep my thermostat at 64° when I'm home and 59° when I'm not. In the summer, I keep it at 74° when I'm home and 77° when I'm not. My air vents are adjusted to keep my bedroom cold around 63° at night, but my bills are never over $120 now (they're about $80 in the winter). Hopefully you're not spending **$1,000 per year** on excessive energy usage.

SMARTPHONE

My family spent over $400 per month for five people to be on a low-speed plan because one person demanded unlimited data. To save over $100 per month, I spent a couple of hours looking at cell phone pricing (wireless providers are very good at confusing people and obfuscating their high prices). I put four of us on a high-speed 4GB plan and the social media addict on a separate low-speed unlimited plan.

Limit your data usage by peeling your face away from your smartphone and engaging with the people around you.

Share a data plan with a few responsible people to save **$50 per month ($600 per year)** each. Have everyone take five minutes to set up automatic payments on Zelle so you don't have to chase them down for money every month.

Also, do you really need the latest smartphone model for $1,000 every 2–3 years? The three-year-old model that's on sale for $100 is still very stylish and has an HD camera, plenty of storage, and high-speed network compatibility. You can use it for 5+ years too. If you don't need to signal higher status with meaningless consumer symbols of identity, older smartphones will save you **$30 per month ($360 per year)**.

CABLE

Your area should have at least two high-speed internet providers. They offer a **$25 per month ($300 per year)** discount for the first 1–2 years, and then they charge full price unless you do something about it. Remember the earlier lessons on negotiating? Call them to renegotiate the price, and if you don't get what you want, switch to the other provider. You could also terminate service under your name and have your roommate or a relative sign up again, but that's technically against the terms of service (if they catch you).

Buy a cable modem and wireless router too. Otherwise, you might have to pay leasing fees and also wait in line with poor people for hours to return equipment.

Hopefully you're using Netflix and other streaming TV. If you're an old couch potato who's befuddled by technology and can't adapt, I'm sorry that you're paying **$50–100 per month ($600–1,200 per year)** for cable TV.

CLOTHING

Millennials and Gen Xers spend $2,000 per year on clothes on average. I spend $500 per year, and I dress better than most men in Asheville (the bar is pretty low here). I have a HORRID fashion sense, and friends used to laugh at me for wearing a cream turtleneck sweater on our Colorado ski trips. I eventually learned to appreciate the aesthetics of minimalism.

My wardrobe consists of a dozen Fred Perry shirts that last 3–5 years, a couple 7 For All Mankind jeans that last 3–5 years, Allen Edmonds boots that last 10+ years (a cobbler recrafts them every 2 years), and a blue jasper bracelet with gold accents from Kartini Studio. I have a couple of nice jackets, some Lululemon workout clothes, and a couple of pairs of Nike shoes too—all bought at 50% discounts online. I would love to hear how you manage to spend more than **$1,000 per year** on clothes.

FURNITURE

When I moved from Chicago to Santa Monica, I spent over $20,000 on new furniture thinking I was a total baller. I sold all of it on Craigslist three years later when I burned out from poker and moved back to Chicago. Being indecisive and never knowing what my life will look like in three years, I spend only $5,000 on new furniture from IKEA or Amazon when I move now.

I'm the last person anyone should consult when it comes to furniture or interior design. But I can save you **$400 per year** on a bed mattress.

I spent thousands of dollars on two Tempur-Pedic mattresses (if you go into a mattress store and the salesman upsells you with, "You spend one-third of your life in bed," just punch him in the dick). One of them was king-size too—big mistake if you live in an apartment because king-size bedding is a pain to launder. I now sleep on a queen-size DreamFoam Ultimate Dreams supreme gel memory foam mattress (buy it on Amazon). It's much cheaper and more comfortable than a high-end Tempur-Pedic.

DOGS

Don't get a dog if you don't have the time, resources, and emotional patience to take care of him! Dogs cost **$2,000 per year** and require 10 hours per week of DIRECT ATTENTION—this means getting off your smartphone and being present when you walk him or play with him.

My dog Rivers was attacked because a bad dog owner thought it was a good idea to bring her anxious pit bulls into the dog park for "socialization." I didn't realize until we got home that they had bitten him. It was a small wound that could've been treated with a saline wash, bandages, and antibiotics, but I took him to the animal hospital to be safe.

I couldn't tell if we were in an animal hospital or a car dealership. The vet came in first to examine Rivers. Then he left the room to talk with his assistant. She came in to show me a treatment bill for $1,000—anesthesia, lab tests, follow-up care, etc. She made the mistake of telling me a few things were optional, and I quickly realized this was a game.

"How am I supposed to afford that?" I responded. She left the room to talk with the vet, then she came back with a $600 bill. "How am I supposed to afford that?" She left the room to talk with the vet, then she came back with a $400 bill. "How am I supposed to afford that?" She finally caved in and asked how much I could afford.

"I brought $150 with me. I might have another $100 at home." I shouldn't have said I had that extra $100 at home. She left the room to talk with the vet, then she came back with a $225 bill. I accepted it even though I could've held out for the last $50–100.

Veterinarians and animal hospitals can extort you if you're not careful. I was hanging out with a different technician at that same hospital. She confirmed that it's standard practice for them to overprescribe treatment. She said that most dog owners don't advocate for themselves by requesting the *minimum effective treatment*. Try to understand what level of treatment is appropriate for your situation to save **$100–500 per year.**

GYM

I used to CrossFit three times per week when my body could handle it. You don't have to spend **$100–200 per**

month ($1,200–2,400 per year) to get into great shape though. You don't need to waste money on personal trainers, supplements, and Fitbits either. Sleep 7–8 hours every night, avoid grains and sugar, and move your body—it's that simple!

Buy a jump rope and a pair of 20-pound dumbbells, and go to the Bodybuilding.com Exercise Finder to learn how to squat, deadlift, row, overhead press, and bench press. Do three sets of each of these five exercises twice per week. Finish with high-intensity cardio—alternate between 30 seconds of intense jump roping and 30 seconds of rest for five minutes. I promise you'll be in phenomenal shape in 6–18 months, and it was FREE!

Dance, yoga, and martial arts are also great. I'm paying $7–10 per class for 2–3 classes per week right now. My local studio offered a six-month challenge membership, which is unlimited classes for $90. They charge you an additional $90 for each month you don't attend at least eight classes though—what a great motivator to get you off your ass! If you're a fat, lazy American who needs to move around, this could save you **$1,000 per year.**

TAXES

Billionaires pay a lower tax rate than you because they've learned the intricacies of our tax system and *legitimately* take advantage of it. I highly recommend using Intuit's TurboTax software for your tax returns. You'll save **$300–400 per year** in tax preparation. You'll eventually learn how to save **$10,000+ per year** through strategic deductions, retirement account contributions, deferred capital gains, tax-loss harvesting, and more.

EDUCATION

Formal education is overrated and nothing more than a babysitting institution. I saved $200,000 by opting out of an MBA in Finance and reading free textbooks used by The Wharton School instead—how do you like them apples? I also built REAL experience by getting my ass kicked in the REAL world.

Unless it's from a top-three school, an MBA or other advanced degree is just expensive toilet paper. Top investment professionals (hedge funds) disregard such credentials, and they focus on who you are (you are not your résumé) and what you've done with your life.

Without any pretentious designations like MBA, CFA, or the laughable CFP, I've had stellar performance over my entire investment track record (perhaps only through sheer luck). As my friend Steve says, "You're either good or you're not," so do whatever it is you do without getting formal permission from some gatekeeper. The lessons you'll learn by being entrepreneurial (but not an entrepreneur—that's an *identity*, not a process) are **priceless**.

ENTERTAINMENT

Yuppies love to eat at expensive restaurants and drink at hotel rooftop bars ($15–20 cocktails!). These places are stuffy and boring! Take a few minutes to stop thinking about how to signal money and status. Think about how to have fun—a hike in the mountains, an escape room, a dance class, an improv comedy show, a brewery, an Ethiopian restaurant. You'll have a way better time and save **$50–200 per week ($2,500–10,000 per year)** too.

When your income is higher than your spending, it's very easy to close that gap with entertainment. I've been known to make it rain at strip clubs when the urge hits (far too often in my twenties). Hopefully you don't fall into a similar spending trap. Save and invest extra money until your savings rate is up to 25–50% (before taxes) first. Then you can splurge all you want on strippers, bottle service, and shiny things if it's important to look like a baller.

ATTRACTION

You are ugly, and that's why you can't save. Above basic needs, most spending is a signal to others of how attractive or how high-status we think we are. Marketers know this, and their advertisements reinforce our insecurity of not feeling good enough. We buy mindless consumer symbols of identity like an Apple logo or Fred Perry wreaths to tell ourselves a story about who we are. I bought a $50,000 sports car when I was 24 because I had low sexual competitiveness and needed to compensate.

Some people preach that you should "just be yourself" because you are perfect as you are. If only it was that easy—some people are just butt-ugly inside and out! Every man and woman can become attractive though if they OWN their ugly and do something about it.

According to *New York Times* best-selling author Tucker Max and evolutionary psychologist Geoffrey Miller in *The*

Mating Grounds podcast, here are some universal traits that influence attraction—

- Empathy and Honesty
- Conscientiousness and Presence
- Intelligence and Open-Mindedness
- Physical Health and Movement
- Emotionality and Happiness
- Courage and Assertiveness
- Verbal and Nonverbal Communication
- Social Resourcefulness
- Material Resourcefulness
- Aesthetic Taste

Your attractiveness isn't just the average of all these traits. For a long time, I thought I could make say $10 million and not need to worry about anything else. But even with some money and a Corvette, I wasn't getting laid.

Your attractiveness is the average of your *three lowest traits*. Material resourcefulness is just ONE TRAIT, and fancy trinkets won't help you plug your leaks. If you put lipstick on a pig, it's still a pig.

People spend a lot of money to hide their ugly. It's not our fault—we've all been manipulated. And it takes years of intense introversion and a healthy lifestyle before we feel comfortable in our own skin.

One day you'll realize that this status competition is not with others. It's with yourself—you move toward your full potential by improving 1% every day. You'll eventually build confidence and be able to signal high status without spending lots of money. In the meantime, just ask yourself before you buy anything, "Does this purchase add real value to my life?"

A QUICK LIFE HACK

My cousin is a high-earning nurse, and she came up with the best strategy for saving that I've ever seen. She doesn't start small with $1,000 per month—she starts BIG. She sets a high savings rate of 50% first, then scales it back *as needed* for living expenses.

She doesn't budget. She doesn't use dumb apps. She simply maxes out her different tax-advantaged retirement accounts—nearly $30,000 per year total. On top of that, she increased her mortgage payments and paid off her house in 10 years.

This automatic process forces her to scale back excessive spending BEFORE it becomes a habit. It's like giving yourself $100 for food and alcohol every week and having to make the best use of it. If she needs more money for spending, she can scale back her investment contributions. But then she'd feel like she's cheating herself out of savings. She hasn't scaled back yet!

I thought my OCD method of thoroughly researching every purchase (it took me two hours to spend $3 on Oral-B Super Floss) saved me a lot of money. Her automatic method is brilliant. "That money is invisible, I put it away, and I don't ever think about it." It's much easier to make good decisions when you structure your life this way!

I've detailed $50,000+ per year in savings ideas in this chapter. If you still can't find $1,000 per month ($12,000 per year) to save for a basic investment plan, then no one can help you. You've given up and identified yourself as a victim, using your dire financial situation as a crutch. It's easy to be a victim and complain about the world. It's hard to take ownership and accountability. It's even harder to overcome inertia and take small steps to improve your life.

The biggest hurdle is your mindset—start thinking for yourself a little bit. Building wealth is easy once you automatically save 25–50% of your income (before taxes), open a few accounts, and make your first trade.

2 | BASIC PLAN

Enough of the tough love and making you feel bad (I swear I'm far less of an asshole in real life)—let's make some money! Here's how you crack the financial system, get rich, and retire early: automatically save 25–50% of your income (before taxes) and invest in low-cost index funds. That's it. This simple solution is detailed in this chapter, and there's not much else you need to know to put yourself in the best position for success.

THE MARKET

When people talk about "the market," they're looking at the U.S. stock market as a whole. It trades on two major stock exchanges, the New York Stock Exchange and the NASDAQ, which list about 4,000 public companies.

Indexes make aggregate tracking of all these stocks easier. Established over 100 years ago, The Dow Jones Industrial Average was the first such index, and it reflects 30 of the biggest companies. These 30 companies now only account for 20% of the total value of the U.S. stock market, so we can't call it "the market" anymore (sorry, baby boomers). The Wilshire 5000 includes all 4,000 publicly-listed stocks and is 100% of the total U.S. stock market, but nobody cares about that index.

The S&P 500 index has been around for over 50 years, and it's about 80% of the total value of the U.S. stock market. Comprised of 500 of the largest companies and none of the smaller ones, it's the definitive benchmark in finance. The S&P 500 index is "the market."

CHOICE

I'll give you three different investment choices. There isn't much difference between them, and they're all great. Make one choice and stick with it. You'll needlessly lose money if you're indecisive and you frequently switch between them.

We'll use low-cost exchange-traded funds (ETFs) in all of our investment plans. They're like mutual funds, and you can own every company in an index with one simple purchase. Remember how much work we had to do to save $50,000 per year in the last chapter? When you have $1 million in your investment accounts, ETFs will save you another $50,000 per year with minimal effort. That's why they're better than expensive mutual funds and more expensive financial advisors who use even more expensive mutual funds.

There are thousands of ETFs to choose from. But don't worry—I've narrowed our choices down to nine ETFs (this chapter introduces the first set of three). I promise that you won't find much better investment options than these nine ETFs.

BlackRock, Vanguard, and State Street dominate the ETF industry. With a few exceptions, they all offer their own version of the nine ETFs in this book. I won't list all of them because that'll just confuse you, but feel free to use a duplicate fund (e.g. BlackRock's IVV or Vanguard's VOO instead of State Street's SPY).

Your first choice is between an S&P 500 index fund (**SPY**), a total U.S. stock market index fund (**ITOT**), and a global stock market index fund (**VT**). SPY is large U.S. companies (500 stocks), ITOT is large and small U.S companies (4,000 stocks), and VT is large and small companies in developed and emerging markets around the world (8,000 stocks). VT is half U.S. companies and half international companies.

You can't go wrong with any of these three choices. The S&P 500 index is what everyone compares against, so choose SPY if you want zero deviation from that benchmark. I prefer the total U.S. stock market (ITOT) over the S&P 500 index (SPY) because small stocks make a little more money than large stocks. You won't notice a difference between ITOT and SPY though.

International stocks also make a little more money than U.S. stocks, but the risk of the global stock market (VT) is slightly higher. It'll sometimes have large deviations from the S&P 500 index (SPY). And if you buy it in an IRA, foreign taxes will eat up a tiny amount—0.05–0.1% per year. But VT is still my preferred investment. If it's hard to decide right now, just use the total U.S. stock market (ITOT).

TRADITIONAL OR ROTH

There's a lot of debate as to whether **Traditional** (pre-tax) or **Roth** (post-tax) is best for your 401(k) plan. I'll give you a simple answer.

If you're in a low tax bracket (10% and 12%), use Roth because you'll pay less tax now than when you move into a higher bracket later. If you're in a high tax bracket (32%

or higher), use Traditional because you'll pay less tax later in retirement when you move down to a lower bracket.

Most people are in a middle tax bracket (22% and 24%). Use a Roth only if you *know for sure* that you'll never be in a low tax bracket—you might be in a low tax bracket for several years if you lose or take a break from your corporate job, start a new business, or retire early. Roth is beneficial if the government raises tax rates in the future. But the free option to convert your Traditional retirement account balances to Roth in low-income years is more important.

You could also make contributions to a Traditional or Roth IRA (Individual Retirement Account) if your income falls below certain thresholds. The rules are complicated and the contribution limit is small ($6,000 per year, plus another $1,000 for old people), so we'll use a Roth IRA only for **conversions** in this book.

BASIC PLAN

1. If you still have an employer and they match your **401(k)** contributions—

    a. Enroll in the 401(k) plan and contribute the maximum that allows you to take full advantage of that benefit. For example, my last employer matched 7% dollar-for-dollar, so I contributed exactly 7% of each paycheck. [There was a three-year vesting or eligibility period for this bonus. Unable to keep my hubris in check, I quit my job three months too soon and told corporate America to shove that $25,000 bonus up their ass. Oops!] Some employers only match 50 cents on the dollar, but you should still max out because that's an easy 50% gain!

b. Every 401(k) plan has an S&P 500 or total U.S. stock market index fund with an expense ratio of less than 0.05% ($50 per $100,000) per year. Allocate 100% of your contributions to that fund. [If you want global exposure, you could allocate 60% to a U.S. stock index fund and 40% to an international "ex-U.S." stock index fund.] You might be tempted to choose a target retirement date fund (a "2050" fund if you're 35 years old in 2020 for example)—the Additional Topics chapter explains why these are scams.

c. If your employer offers stock options that allow you to buy company shares at a discount, take full advantage of that as well. Sell those shares and buy stock ETFs (ITOT, VT, or SPY) as soon as you can without penalty.

2. Let's assume the current mortgage rate is 3.5%.

   a. If you have loans with interest rates higher than 3.5%, call credit unions and refinance to a lower rate. For loans you can't refinance, pay them off as quickly as possible. Start with the highest interest rate loan, then work your way down.

   b. If you have loans with interest rates lower than 3.5%, keep making regular payments. You usually don't want to pay those off early because you're taking advantage of cheap financing.

   c. Once per year, call credit unions for current auto loan and mortgage rates. Refinance to a lower rate if possible.

   d. Payments for auto loans and for mortgages on homes you live in are considered *spending*. Payments for other loans (credit cards, student debt, mortgages for rental properties) are considered *saving* and count toward the 25–50% target. Don't buy extra cars, a big home, or vacation properties if you want to build wealth!

3. Don't continue until you take advantage of FREE MONEY from employer matching and you pay off ALL of your high-interest loans. In the following steps, let's assume you make $40,000 per year from a part-time employer and $65,000 from a side gig, and you save $50,000 of that income.

4. If you have income from self-employment (either your main job or a side gig) and no employees, go to Fidelity.com and open a **SEP-IRA**. I have no relationship with Fidelity, but they are definitively THE BEST brokerage because they don't charge commissions on ETF trades and they don't sell your orders to high-speed traders who profit at your expense. [If you have employees, call Fidelity at +1 (866) 418–5173 to set up a 401(k).]

5. Link your SEP-IRA to your bank account. The contribution limit is 20% of your *net earnings from self-employment* (net profit × 92.35%). If you make $65,000

from self-employment, send $12,000 ($65,000 × 92.35% × 20%) to your SEP-IRA by setting up an **automatic deposit** of $1,000 every month.

    a. If your net earnings are over $285,000 in any year, your contribution is capped at $57,000. To potentially double this cap to $114,000, add your spouse as an employee of your business and open a SEP-IRA for them.

    b. Your income might fluctuate a lot. Be careful not to contribute more than the 20% or $57,000 limit (whichever is lower). If you accidentally contribute too much, you'll have to file a Return of Excess Contribution form with Fidelity to correct your mistake. If you do this before the tax filing deadline, the IRS won't penalize you.

6. You're about to make your first trade!

    a. Once your $1,000 deposit clears, log in to your Fidelity SEP-IRA when the U.S. stock market is open—Monday through Friday, 9:30 a.m. to 4:00 p.m. EST, excluding holidays.

b. Click the **Trade** button to open a trade window. You'll see that you have $1,000 in **Cash Available to Trade**. Leave the **Transaction Type** box as **Stocks/ETFs**. Type *ITOT* (for the total U.S. stock market index fund) or *VT* (for the global stock market index fund) or *SPY* (for the S&P 500 index fund) in the **Symbol** box, then select **Buy** in the **Action** box.

c. The current prices of that ETF will now appear. Divide your available cash by the current **Ask** (the price you can buy at), then round down to the nearest whole number. Type that into the **Quantity** box. For example, if you have $1,000 and the **Ask** is $67.00, you'll buy 14 shares. There's also a **Calculate Quantity** button if you're lazy.

d. Set the **Order Type** box to **Market Order**, and *make sure the U.S. stock market is open!* Also avoid the first and last half hour of the trading day because of higher volatility (prices move around a lot). Leave the **Time in Force** box as **Day**.

e. Click the **Preview Order** button, then double- and triple-check the details of your order. Make sure it's a **Buy** order and NOT a Sell order—many investment professionals (including yours truly) still make this mistake.

f. Click the **Place Order** button. Your order will be filled by a seller immediately. Thanks to Fidelity, you'll often get a better price—maybe $66.995 instead of $67.00.

7. Congratulations, you just made your first trade! That wasn't so scary, was it? This is where rookies start making mistakes—they sell early or they wait to buy. Whatever price the stock market is showing on any given day, I promise you it's fair. Buy stocks (ITOT, VT, or SPY) as soon as your deposits clear every month. Don't ever try to time the market because it'll cost you a lot of money in the long run!

8. Wait two trading days for the money to officially settle. Log in to Fidelity.com, select your **SEP-IRA**, click the **Account Features** tab, click **Brokerage & Trading** to expand a menu of options, and click **Dividends and Capital Gains**. The full name of your

stock index fund will be listed here. Click the **Update** link at the end of that row. For **Dividends** and **Capital Gains**, click the options under **Reinvest in Security**. Also check the two boxes underneath so that any payments (interest, dividends, and capital gains) from your current and future investments are automatically reinvested.

9. If you still have an employer and they offer a 401(k) plan, the contribution limit is currently $19,500 per year. Max that out at $750 per paycheck if you get paid every two weeks. Old people (specifically over 50) can contribute another $6,500 per year.

10. If you make much less than $285,000, save much more than 20%, and don't contribute to a 401(k), you might want to open a **Solo 401(k)** instead of a SEP-IRA. It allows you to contribute $19,500 PLUS 20% of your remaining net earnings. The cap is $57,000 total, and you can add your spouse to double the limits. It's a lot of extra paperwork upfront and every year, but call Fidelity at +1 (800) 544-5373 if you want this account.

11. Open a second account with Fidelity—a taxable **Brokerage Account.** Compared to a 401(k) and IRAs,

this account won't give you tax benefits that equate to a bonus of roughly 1% per year. But it's still necessary (most of my wealth is in a Brokerage Account, but that's because I'm an idiot and didn't take advantage of IRAs when I was younger). Repeat steps 4 through 8 but for a Brokerage Account, and send the rest of your savings to this account. If you save $50,000 per year with $12,000 going to your SEP-IRA and $19,500 going to your 401(k), set up an **automatic deposit** of $1,542 per month (about $18,500 per year) into your Brokerage Account.

12. When you leave an employer, do a **Direct Rollover** of the entire balance of your 401(k) into your SEP-IRA. Any checks should be made out to Fidelity **For Benefit Of** your IRA. Never do an Indirect Transfer! Select the option to liquidate your investments and transfer it all over in cash. Once it clears, buy shares of new investments (ITOT, VT, or SPY) right away. Don't stress yourself by sitting on this large cash balance and waiting for the perfect time to enter the market. I tried to do this on my first rollover of $500,000. It drove me crazy and shattered my confidence for months!

13. If you receive a sudden windfall (inheritance, gambling winnings, lawsuit settlement, etc.), put ALL of that money in your Brokerage Account. Invest it right away—100% in stocks (ITOT, VT, or SPY) if it's a small amount, maybe 60% in stocks and 40% in bonds if it's a large amount (skip to the Intermediate Plans). Do not sit on cash!

14. There will be years where you can take advantage of low tax brackets (10% and 12% currently). Open a third account with Fidelity—a **Roth IRA**. During low-income years, do a **Partial Conversion** of your **SEP-IRA**—enough to take full advantage of low tax brackets. In 2020 for example, the cutoff for the 12% bracket is $40,125, plus a $12,400 standard deduction. With no income, credits, or other deductions, you should convert $52,525 that year (you should actually convert $49,960 to qualify for Obamacare). You'd pay $4,617.50 in federal taxes now ($9,875 × 10% + [$40,125 - $9,875] × 12%), but that's way less than the $11,555.50 ($52,525 × 22%) or more you'd pay later when you have real income! Repeat step 8 for your Roth IRA as well to automatically reinvest payments.

15. Let's mitigate taxes some more. Log in to Fidelity.com, select your **Brokerage Account**, click the **Account Features** tab, click **Brokerage & Trading** to expand a menu of options, and click **Cost Basis Information Tracking**. Click the **Change** link next to where it says First In, First Out (FIFO), select the **Tax-Sensitive** option, click **Save**, and click **OK**. If you're not using Fidelity, **Maximize Short-Term Loss** is a good option with other brokerages.

16. Don't touch the money in these accounts until you're retired! Don't take 401(k) loans. Don't make early withdrawals. Don't use it for the down payment on a home, medical expenses, or education. I don't care if you lose your job and over 30% of your savings because of the coronavirus. It may take 3–7 years, but the market ALWAYS recovers! Your 401(k) and IRAs are protected from bankruptcy and creditors (with a few exceptions like the IRS), so don't be shy about filing for bankruptcy if you're experiencing hardship. You can go broke and still be a millionaire!

    a. Calculate your annual living expenses, then subtract social security if you're 62 or older, pension if you're 55, and other benefits. If that number is more than 3% of your savings balance (some say 4%, but that's aggressive—you'll run out of money if you live a long life), you're not ready to retire. Go back to work or develop better habits around money.

b. You can take distributions (withdrawals) from your 401(k) and IRAs without penalty starting at the age of 59½ (I want to punch the idiot who couldn't just round it to 60). Don't touch these accounts—take advantage of their tax benefits as long as you can! From 59½ to 72, withdraw what you need for expenses only from your Brokerage Account. Also remember to take advantage of Roth IRA conversions in low tax brackets.

c. Once you turn 72, take the **Required Minimum Distribution (RMD)** every year. Don't neglect this; otherwise, you'll pay a 50% penalty! With sufficient IRA balances (you should've rolled over every 401(k) into your IRAs), this payout schedule gives you plenty of money to live on for the first 20 years. If you need more, withdraw from your Brokerage Account.

d. The 10% early withdrawal penalty is the best feature of the 401(k) and IRAs. Aside from hoarding toilet paper in a pandemic, we're not evolved to be good at saving resources (our hunter-gatherer ancestors would find the idea of retirement preposterous). And just like the inevitability of eating junk food in your pantry, it's far too easy to tap into your Brokerage Account and use that money for something else. There isn't a lock to keep your hands out of that account. Try hard not to eat the cookie sitting in front of you. Wait until retirement, then you'll have 10 cookies!

17. Investing all of your savings in stocks is **high-risk**, and you can lose 30% or more in a very bad year! $250,000 isn't a lot of money though. And if you're saving at least $2,000 per month, you'll replenish your accounts quickly in all but the worst market downswings. Get your savings rate up to 25–50% of your income (before taxes) first. Once your annual contributions total less than 10% of your wealth (for example, you save $50,000 per year and the total of your 401(k), IRAs, and Brokerage Account is over $500,000), then you can think about protecting your money with some bonds.

3 | INTERMEDIATE CONCEPTS

I bet I can anticipate every mistake you'll make. This chapter shows you what you're doing wrong and how to minimize the damage.

COMPOUNDING AND RISK

You learned about compound interest in middle school. If you invest $100,000 upfront and make *exactly* 10% every year, you'll have more than $200,000 at the end of 10 years—$259,374 to be precise. The longer you invest, the stronger the effect of compounding.

There's no guarantee you'll have exactly $259,374 because markets are risky. NOBODY can predict how technology, violence, disease, or anything else will change the world. At the end of 10 years, you might have as much as $400,000 or as little as $100,000.

Also, the *benchmark* might be 10% per year, but calling it "expected return" is misleading. You should have NO EXPECTATIONS for what you'll make in any single year. ANYTHING CAN HAPPEN—sear this into your brain!

Risk is somewhat mitigated over time. It's easy to be unlucky for one decade, but it's hard to be unlucky three decades in a row. At the end of 30 years, you'll have between $1.5 million and $2 million in this fantasy example.

Growth of 10% per year is unrealistic, so let's use a more practical number. If you save $2,000 per month ($24,000 per year) and grow at 5% per year over 30 years, you'll retire with $1–2 million. That's not great, as you'll only be able to live on $30,000–60,000 per year. *After inflation*, that's like living on $20,000–40,000 this year.

If you save $4,000 per month ($48,000 per year), that gets you to $2–4 million. You don't want any less than this for retirement, especially if you have a family. You'll live on $60,000–120,000 per year. *After inflation*, that's like living on $40,000–80,000 this year.

That's still not much, but you'll also have social security and maybe pension benefits. Get that savings rate up if you want to retire in less than 30–40 years!

Inflation and medical expenses are risky variables too. Save more than you could ever need so you can be secure in your retirement.

STOCK MARKET RETURN

You've probably heard that the market returned an average of 10–12% per year. That's technically true, but you'll be disappointed if you have the same expectations going forward.

First of all, there's a big difference between the average return and the actual growth rate. Let's say you make 100% on $100,000 in year 1 and now have $200,000. Then you lose 50% in year 2 and are back down to $100,000. The *average* of a 100% gain and a 50% loss is +25% per year. But you broke even, so your growth rate was actually +0%! The *compound annual growth rate* of the market was 7–9%, not 10–12%.

Secondly, U.S. interest rates averaged 3–4% per year historically. We're now below 1%, and we'll be there for a while.

Lastly, the historical equity risk premium, which is the stock market return minus the interest rate, averaged 6% per year. This was over a period that averaged 3% for inflation and growth. Forward estimates of inflation and growth are 2%, so your compensation for taking risk is now only 4%.

A long-term interest rate of 1–2% plus an equity risk premium of 4% means you should calibrate your expectations down to **5–6% per year**. This might feel like a real kick in the balls, but you were only making 7–9% before. Inflation that's 1% lower is also like adding 1% to your return (lower inflation makes everything cheaper when you finally get to spend that money). And don't forget the 1% tax benefit of retirement accounts!

Average investors will make mistakes (trading, market timing, financial advisors, etc.) and earn only 0–2% per year on their wealth. You can make 5–6% and rub it in their face!

EMERGENCY FUND

Many people keep 3–12 months of living expenses in a bank account for emergencies. You don't need to do this—1–2 months of living expenses is all you need.

Don't let a large cash balance sit idly in accounts that earn less than 0.1% interest per year. You can find an online bank like Marcus that often pays 1–2% more. You could also pay off debt and save on 3–4% interest. Or you could just invest in stocks and bonds, make 3–6%, take advantage of lower *capital gains* tax rates and deferred capital gains (paying taxes much later), and figure out your life as you go.

What constitutes an emergency anyway? If your dog needs surgery or your home needs a major repair, you can reduce your savings rate for a few months or sell some stocks in your Brokerage Account. If the market crashes (loses 20% or more) at the same time you lose your job, you can collect unemployment benefits while you get back on your feet.

The biggest drawback of an emergency fund isn't its low interest. What happens when you have easy access to money? You spend it. When you lose your job, it's not an emergency fund—it's a crutch. You'll get lazy, you won't develop new skills, and you won't make an effort to go back to work. The longer your cushy emergency fund keeps you in inertia, the harder it will be to get off your ass and do something with your life.

I quit my job as an oil trader to become a professional poker player. With $100,000 in cash, I was a glorified bum without an upward trajectory for four years. I have several friends who left their jobs and lived this Bohemian lifestyle with me as well. Don't let this happen to you!

HEALTH SAVINGS ACCOUNT (HSA)

Not to be confused with an FSA (flexible spending account), an HSA looks great on the surface. It combines the pre-tax benefit of a Traditional retirement account with the post-tax benefit of a Roth. But you *must* pair it with a high deductible health plan.

Remember that I advocate a min/max strategy for insurance—

- Either opt for full coverage if you get subsidies through work or Obamacare, especially if you have health issues (max);

- Or consider going without health insurance if you're young, healthy, and don't receive subsidies (min).

High deductible health plans are awful. They're half the cost of full coverage, and they only kick in when there's a catastrophe.

I was on a high deductible health plan for years. On top of the $150–200 per month premium, I would also pay hundreds of dollars out-of-pocket for primary doctor visits, lab tests, and asthma prescriptions (which I don't need anymore—probably never needed—because I make an effort to stay healthy).

I had an unknown throat issue that freaked me out. I thought it could've been everything from bone spurs to hyperthyroidism (never listen to idiot speculators on the internet). I flew back to Chicago for specialists, x-rays, an endoscopy, and an ultrasound. They found NOTHING—it was all in my head (stress and paranoia)! Shockingly, my insurance didn't cover any of this, and I had to pay thousands of dollars more.

Why pay lots of money for something that will rarely benefit you? I can't recommend an HSA because the required high deductible health plan is useless. The one rare exception is if you're employed, they pay half of your health insurance, they match your HSA contributions, and you're healthy.

THE 529 PLAN

I don't recommend the 529 or other college savings plans either, and here's why—

- Your IRAs already give you tax benefits and allow you to withdraw for college expenses.

- These plans aren't required to disclose their fees, which could be high. They might also force you to invest in expensive mutual funds instead of low-cost index funds.

- It's impossible to calculate exactly how much you'll need for college in 20 years. Any excess is subject to higher income tax (instead of lower capital gains tax) and a 10% penalty.

You'll also pay that higher tax and penalty if—

- You later decide to keep that money for yourself because your children turn into entitled suburban shits.

- Your children don't go to college because they're inbred or lazy.

- Your children go to massage, acupuncture, or some other trade school because they're anti-capitalist hippies.

- You're a tiger parent and you breed high-achieving trophy children like me. They'll grow up insular and antisocial, and it'll be hard for them to relate to others. They'll rebel against you, decide formal education and corporate slave labor are beneath them, and pursue more entrepreneurial endeavors.

Use a 529 plan only for private K–12 education, where you can withdraw a maximum of $10,000 per year. From the time they're born, invest no more than $500 per month ($6,000 per year) per child for this purpose. If you earn 5–6% per year from a low-cost stock index fund, you'll deplete each account around the time they graduate high school.

FUN MONEY

I'd tell you to strictly adhere to the Basic and Intermediate Plans in this book and never deviate from them, but you wouldn't listen to me. You'll use fancy charts to time market entry and exit points. You'll pick stocks that a coworker supposedly made money from because his revisionist history is infallible. You'll dick around with call and put options because you interact with morons on Reddit.

For many people, the only way they'll ever learn is by walking the dark path on their own. That's certainly true for me. When I jumped back into finance, I had to lose 40% of my startup capital before I gave up day trading.

We learn best through feeling and emotion, and the amygdala is responsible for storing memories with help from the hippocampus and prefrontal cortex. I have elephant gonad–sized amygdalae, which is why I'm hyperemotional and like a tempest in a teapot. But I remember everything.

We don't learn well through cold logic and memorization of boring facts. I could spew all the right answers to you, but you won't learn unless you *feel* through story or experience. What do you remember from college? Did you learn anything useful from assigned textbooks and class lectures?

Open a second Brokerage Account and allocate **10%** of your savings there. This is your fun money trading account—do whatever you want with it. You'll need 10,000 hours of deliberate practice with a good feedback system to develop some intuition with the stock market. During this time, don't try to make sense of the price movements—just observe.

If you don't have 10,000 hours to learn investment finance, come back to the Basic and Intermediate Plans in this book. You'll eventually make enough mistakes to realize that you can't beat the market.

Some brokerages offer paper money trading accounts where you play with fake money. Don't waste your time with these simulated accounts. They don't reflect actual trading conditions accurately. Even worse, they'll give you a false sense of confidence.

I quit my career as a professional poker player to day trade because of a paper money account. I thought the thousands of fictitious dollars I was raking in every day meant I could compete with real professionals. If your gut tells you something is too good to be true, listen to it.

INVEST IN YOURSELF

This next point trumps everything else in the book. The best investment you can make is IN YOURSELF! The second best investment you can make is in your friends and family and the local community around you.

I'll save you 9,995 hours of your life. Read this book in 5 hours—you don't need to waste any more time with finance. Thinking about money only distracts you from what's important.

Your career and relationships are important, but so are hobbies. Redirect **10%** of your income toward developing skills and taking on new challenges. Psychology, improv comedy, and dance are a few of my hobbies. If you don't have time to enjoy your life, find the time. I don't care what your excuse is.

These extracurricular activities won't provide an immediate return on investment. They'll pay massive dividends in the future though—way more than stocks and bonds. But you must be *fully engaged* to benefit from them (show up to your own life!).

DIVERSIFY YOUR LIFE

I'll briefly take you down a transcendental rabbit hole to buttress the importance of investing in yourself. The legendary Japanese swordsman Miyamoto Musashi once said, "From one thing, know ten thousand things." Let's map the 68–95–99 rule in statistics on top of that.

If you want to improve yourself and reach 68% of your potential, master one thing. If you want to reach 95% of your potential, master two things. If you want to reach 99% of your potential, master three things. This is how you discover purpose and start to understand the truth of the universe.

The reason for such large overlap is because mastery at any one thing requires mastery of self, mastery of others, and mastery of that domain. Someone who understands their emotions, relates well to others, and has technical expertise in their field can apply their skills elsewhere. Someone who's mastered three different fields can apply their skills EVERYWHERE.

The three fields need to be unrelated though. I mastered video games as a child. I mastered poker as a young adult. I mastered finance as an adult. But these three things are highly correlated. That's why I'm still immature and have a narrow-minded, utilitarian view of the world.

You might be feeling unfulfilled because you have a boring, domesticated life that's just work and family. Diversify your life instead of being physically or verbally violent toward your spouse and kids. If one aspect of your life should fail (every aspect of your life is likely to fail at some point—divorce is a lucrative business for attorneys), other pieces will make it easier to put yourself back together.

TUNE OUT ALL THE BULLSHIT!

There's so much noise in the world today. I rarely log in to Facebook, my only social media account, so I can avoid the constant signals of moral virtue and moral outrage that pollute my feed. I set my phone to permanently silent so I can ignore people who blow it up with the EXPECTATION of an immediate response. As an investment professional, I spend no more than 15 minutes reading market news, and I look at asset prices only once per day. Why? Because whatever's happening in the world, IT DOESN'T MATTER!

Take a moment to think about how much useless information you consume every day. If you care about your wealth and your health, tune out ALL OF IT. Turn off CNBC and other financial media. Ignore everyone's dumb stock and bitcoin advice. Tell financial advisors to piss off. Delete stock apps and personal finance podcasts from your phone.

I used to watch CNBC, listen to traders, and stare at charts all day because I thought that conferred high status. All of these things are just counterproductive **NOISE**. If you want to make money from investing, the ONLY thing that matters is good habits.

EGO DEPLETION

We only have so much self-control or willpower available to make decisions and act effectively each day. Small wins (like a nice smile) and small losses (like a mean Facebook comment) can add to or subtract from our willpower. Because of our fight-or-flight response system, losses affect us more than wins. One big loss can deplete your willpower just as quickly as six small losses. When you've reached this state of ego depletion, you have to reset and call it a day.

I tried to day trade for half a year, and I watched my profits and losses fluctuate by hundreds of dollars from one minute to the next. The stock market has yet to lose six years in a row (it came very close once). It's uncommon for it to lose six months in a row. It's not uncommon for it to lose six days in a row. It loses six minutes in a row on most days.

If your confidence and identity are tied to one thing and that one thing picks up negative momentum, you'll get depressed often. This is especially true for me because I need constant external validation.

What do you think happened when I stared at my computer screen for eight hours—minute by minute, tick by tick, inevitably facing a barrage of small losses? Imagine hitting six consecutive red lights when you're already late for work EVERY SINGLE DAY. It drove me crazy! I was so miserable and frustrated that I would frequently shut off all my monitors, crawl into a dark closet, and relieve the tension by watching porn. *Buy, buy, buy; sell, sell, sell; JACK, JACK, JACK!*

Good investing is counterintuitive to every emotional instinct. The harder you try, the quicker you'll burn out. If you walk down the middle of the road, one foot in front of the other until you reach the finish line, you'll make lots of money. If you panic and run back and forth between one side of the road and the other, you'll get run over. Don't play *Frogger* with your money—the slow, boring tortoise wins this race.

Invest your savings as soon as the money is available (the best time to invest is always RIGHT NOW), and don't look at your statements more than once per year. You don't need to pay attention to the market, which will only induce ego depletion, anger, and lots of mistakes. I reported profits and losses to my dad EVERY DAY when I lived in his basement, and he would occasionally yell at me after a string of small losses. Instead of following the market, spend that time filling each day with six small wins.

DRAWDOWNS AND THE 20% RULE

If you had all your money in stocks during the 2008 financial crisis, you would've lost over 50% from October 9, 2007, to March 9, 2009. You also would've lost 50% from September 3, 1929, to July 8, 1932 (the Dow index had a 90% drawdown during the Great Depression, but you would've picked up 20–30% in dividends and 10–20% from deflation). Not that you're tracking daily profits and losses or watching CNBC, but you still know you're losing a lot of money. And it's painful. You can expect a few more of these big drawdowns over your lifetime.

I've already had three 50% drawdowns as an adult—all from spending. I was eliminated on the first day of the 2009 World Series of Poker championship, I lost another $10,000 in side games, and then I blew $50,000 on a new car a few months later. Fortunately, I was making a lot of money and had a 50% savings rate.

The first six months after moving to Los Angeles, I spent $50,000 on furniture and excessive living expenses, I was lazy and didn't work much, and I tried to dominate poker on new turf, losing another $20,000 right away. During my time there, my savings rate was 0% because I worked only enough hours to cover expenses.

When I moved back to Chicago, I lived off of savings, I hired a personal chef and had other ridiculous expenses, and I was exceedingly risky with my personal investments (if you think a 100% allocation to stocks is risky, imagine 200%!). With a savings rate of –500% (I spent FIVE TIMES MORE than my realistic income), I lived way above my means. I then lost a lot of money when the bond market went through a down cycle in 2015.

Losing half your money is depressing. I moved back in with my parents for a few years and vowed to never let that happen again.

20% drawdowns on our wealth are also painful, and we don't want them to happen too often. The stock market loses 30% in a very bad year. If you have less than $250,000 in the stock market, you don't need to worry. Your wealth will be replenished by $50,000 per year in savings.

Let's call that $50,000 a 20% *replenish rate* ($50,000 divided by $250,000) even though it might be a savings rate of 50% ($50,000 divided by $100,000 per year income). When your savings rate is 25–50% (before taxes) and your replenish rate dips below **10%** (i.e. when your $250,000 grows to $500,000 in this example), we'll start investing in bonds to protect your wealth and limit 20% drawdowns.

MEMENTO MORI

What else can we do about risk? First understand that volatility and drawdowns are a natural part of the process. Whether it's an inflation spook, a pandemic, or a presidential election, everything moves in cycles. The WORST thing you can do is overreact and make big changes to your investment strategy (i.e. sell ALL of your stocks) every time the wind blows. Like a ship captain in a storm, you can't control nature. All you can do is pay attention to feedback and make small adjustments along the way (rebalancing).

Baby boomers working in factories and steel mills in the Midwest are a dying breed. They think life is a straight line that goes up and to the right. That's fine if your goal is to subsist for 10 years while a quickly evolving world kills you slowly (inflation).

We know that life isn't a straight line—at times we crack only to let the light in. Drawdowns can be a blessing because we **learn how to lose**, and that which doesn't kill us makes us stronger. Your muscles grow bigger when you test their limits through weight training. And with injuries, you recover through movement, tension, and stress (not a glut of Western medicine).

The WORST thing that can happen when you dick around in your fun money trading account, play in the World Series of Poker, or buy a lottery ticket is that you WIN. You'll directly tie your actions to random results, and for the *rest of your life* you'll think you're a god. You'll continue making big mistakes—no one will be able to tell you otherwise—and you'll go broke (financially AND emotionally).

I've never been lucky in any aspect of my life, and I've failed in most endeavors. Where I'm luckier than most though is that I've NEVER had it easy. If I ever had it easy—if I had won the 2009 World Series of Poker championship or made millions from day trading—some would call that success. But I know with certainty that I'd be a FAILURE right now, which is much worse than just failing.

The idea of memento mori evolved with early Christianity, and it translates to: "remember that you will die." Most of our accomplishments are meaningless because we all die eventually. The only thing that matters is how you CHOOSE to live your life—in acceptance or fear? If you live in fear, you're already dead.

Poker players believe it's bad luck to play a few more hands when their chips are in the rack and they're about to leave. If they're winning, they'll play scared for the last half hour or the last few hands. I used to be this way too, and I've folded AK (one of the best possible hands) a few times. You can't avoid the inevitable, and far too often we would get stung with a big loss right at the end of the night because we cared too much.

At some point I started not caring if I finished the day on a downswing. If I felt an urge to fold strong hands, I would chant to myself, "Remember that you will die," and push through that fear. I know it's statistically impossible, but ever since I made this mental switch, it feels like I've finished on an upswing *ten times* more often than a downswing! I've also destroyed plenty of other players as they were about to leave, and there are threads on the 2+2 poker forums describing how I've crushed young men's dreams.

You're going to suffer no matter what you decide to do. And if you fear to play out of the rack, you WILL make your own bad luck. It's better to recognize and accept suffering and to let down cycles have their place than to try to control everything. Always focus on a solid **process**. Don't frantically obsess over the *results* and what you could've done with perfect hindsight. How well do you think you'll do as an investor if you let fear control your decisions?

Even with two massive drawdowns, two world wars, and other periods of turmoil, the stock market persevered through ALL OF IT and gained 7–9% per year. If you try to control the chaos by constantly jumping in and out of the stock market, you'll get run over. If you try to avoid the chaos by hoarding cash in a bank account, inflation will kill you. But if you learn to **embrace the chaos** and take on a little bit of risk, I swear you will reap plenty of riches that this world has to offer.

2020 CORONAVIRUS CRISIS

I lost hundreds of thousands of dollars in the coronavirus pandemic (a 30% drawdown at its nadir). This was way more money than I had ever lost, and I'm responsible for friends and family too. I tried to catch a falling knife by rebalancing (trimming profitable bonds and buying cheap stocks) four days ahead of schedule. I stared at my trading screens for the next four days, and each hour that passed felt like a punch in the gut. I thought I could time the market, but all I did was induce ego depletion and lose $25,000 on the early rebalance.

Other than that one trade, I haven't lost sleep over this market crash. On days the market dropped 10%, I didn't bat an eye. I've been relaxed and optimistic throughout this entire ordeal. How? I have a solid long-term investment process, I tune out all the bullshit, and I **ZOOM OUT** and look at the big picture—

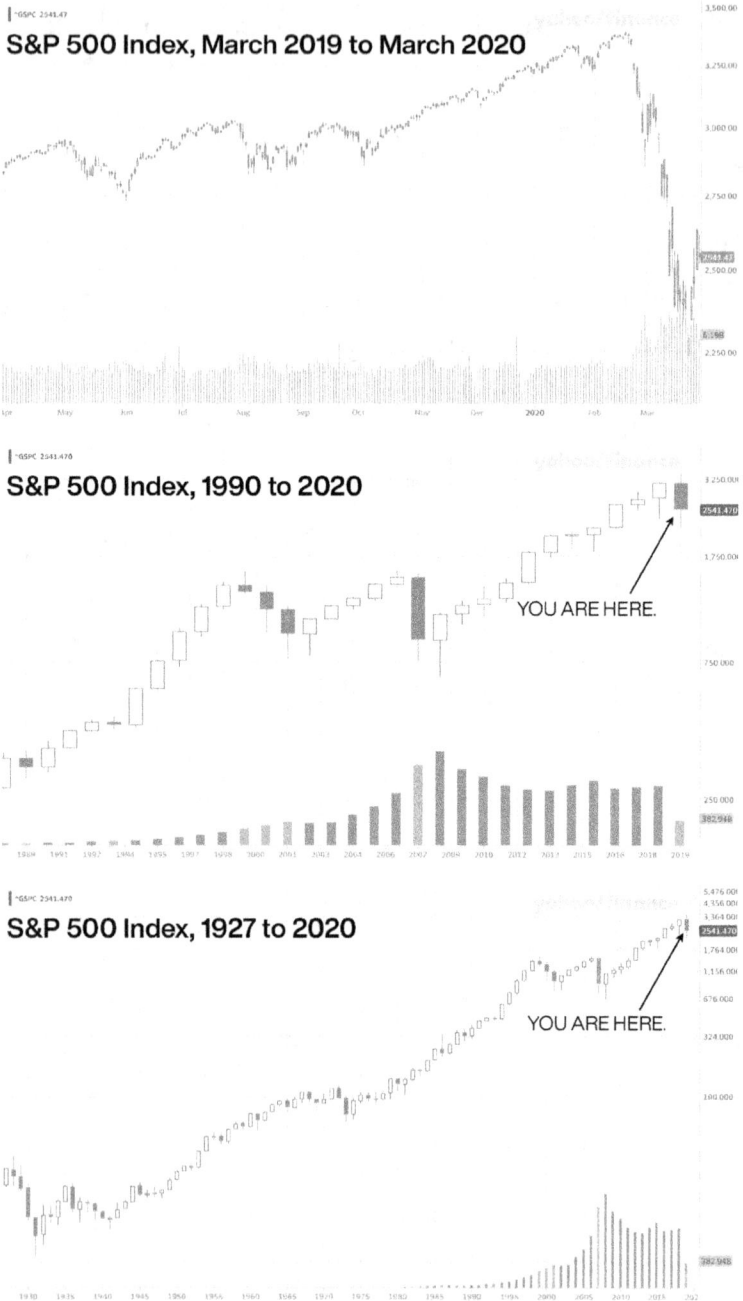

Nothing is as important as you think it is while you're going through it—not the coronavirus, not a Trump presidency, not anything. There will always be something that could make the market spaz. There will always be risk. OWN IT, or live in fear forever!

4 | INTERMEDIATE PLANS

If you don't have at least $250,000 (equity on homes you live in doesn't count), you're still poor. You should be saving 25–50% of your income (before taxes), and you should have enough saved that your replenish rate is below 10% (for example, you save $50,000 per year and the total of your 401(k), IRAs, and Brokerage Account is over $500,000). If you're not there, get there first. You need to build good money habits and understand risk before you can continue.

You'll reduce risk as your wealth grows from now on. You'll never increase your market risk as you get older.

SHORT-TERM TREASURY BILLS

Americans have most of their wealth in retirement and brokerage accounts, a primary home and other real estate, private business investments, and checking and savings accounts. Many people keep a lot of cash in bank accounts that don't pay much interest.

Instead of holding cash, you could buy shares of a short-term Treasury bill index fund (**BIL**). Treasury bills are 1- to 12-month bonds issued by the U.S. government, and they offer competitive interest rates. Unlike savings accounts, interest earned on Treasuries is exempt from state and local taxes. Short-term Treasury bills have basically zero risk, and you'll earn 1–2% per year in the long run.

AGGREGATE BONDS

There's a lot of confusion when it comes to bonds. Long, complicated textbooks have been written to explain what they are, what they do, and how they're priced.

Here's an easier way to look at them—bonds are IOUs (I owe you) that are issued by governments and corporations (borrowers) so they can use money (principal) from others (lenders) for a fixed amount of time (term). Borrowers pay interest (rate) to lenders every month or every year, and they return the principal at the end of the term. Lenders can buy and sell these IOUs to other lenders (investors) in the bond market.

Interest rates on bonds are where they're confusing. Let's say you receive an IOU for loaning a friend $10,000 to buy a car at an interest rate of 1% for one year (we'll assume he never defaults). He'll owe you $10,100 in a year. If the market interest rate goes up to 2% immediately after you give him money, the IOU isn't worth as much. You could write the same IOU and receive $10,200 in a year instead of $10,100. If the market interest rate drops to 0%, the IOU is worth more because you're receiving $10,100 instead of $10,000.

Bonds fall in value when interest rate expectations go up and rise in value when interest rate expectations go down. Bonds fall in value when interest rate expectations go up and rise in value when interest rate expectations go down. Bonds fall in value when interest rate expectations go up and rise in value when interest rate expectations go down. Got it?

Long-term interest rate expectations are currently 1–2% (that's what's already "priced-in"). You won't lose money in bonds when interest rates rise from historic lows of 0% to those expectations of 1–2% in 10–30 years. You'll lose money if long-term interest rate expectations rise to 3–4%. You'll make extra money if we stay near 0% for a very long time.

The Federal Reserve is the central bank of the U.S., and they control the supply of money. When the economy is running hot and we're all making money, they'll raise interest rates to cool it down and build in some protection against hard times. If there's a threat of a recession, they'll aggressively lower interest rates to stimulate the economy. For a 30-minute explanation of what I just said, go to YouTube and watch *How the Economic Machine Works* by Ray Dalio (it's an excellent primer on economics).

We'll use an aggregate bond index fund (**AGG**) in this playbook. It's a collection of low-risk (investment grade) bonds, and it includes Treasuries, mortgage-backed securities, and corporate bonds. An aggregate bond fund has some risk, but it's far less risky than the stock market. It earns roughly 1% more per year than short-term Treasury bills.

MORTGAGE-BACKED SECURITIES

Instead of using all the bonds in an aggregate bond fund, we could just invest in mortgage-backed securities (a large bundle of home loans) through a low-cost index fund (**VMBS**). As people pay down their mortgages, you'll collect payments that are roughly 1% higher than short-term Treasury bills. These bonds are also backed by the U.S. government if homeowners default.

Do not confuse these low-risk mortgage-backed securities (AAA credit rating) with *subprime* mortgages (A-, B, C, and D credit ratings) that induced the 2008 financial crisis (go watch *The Big Short*, starring Christian Bale, Steve Carell, Ryan Gosling, and Brad Pitt). VMBS is slightly less risky than AGG, and you won't lose as much if inflation or interest rates go up.

CHOICE

I prefer mortgage-backed securities, but the choice between aggregate bonds (AGG), mortgage-backed securities (VMBS), and short-term Treasury bills (BIL) is up to you. You can't go wrong with any of them. If it's hard to decide right now, just use aggregate bonds (AGG).

INTERMEDIATE 60/40 PLAN

1. You generally need $250,000 in your Fidelity accounts before they invite you to participate in their Fully Paid Lending Program. Call a representative at +1 (800) 343-3548, and they'll send you a form to

activate this feature. Securities lending allows you to pick up a little bit of free money from your ETFs by making your shares available for others to borrow or short. To be clear, you'll still own these shares and any profits and losses until you sell them.

2. You might have as little as $250,000 or as much as $1 million, and most of it should be in IRAs and a Brokerage Account. If you have a 401(k) with an old employer, roll it over to your SEP-IRA. We'll leave our stock investments alone and buy bonds from now on.

3. Mortgage-backed securities are never an option in 401(k) plans, and the stable value (money market) fund is always expensive. Allocate all future contributions to the aggregate U.S. bond index fund with an expense ratio of less than 0.05% ($50 per $100,000) per year. Be careful not to invest in high yield or junk bond funds—these are advanced *credit* investments that act like stocks.

4. Bonds are better off in retirement accounts to avoid their higher tax rate. We'll slowly shift stocks from your IRAs to your Brokerage Account. Let's say you

have $3,000 per month ($36,000 per year) going into your SEP-IRA and $2,000 per month ($24,000 per year) going into your taxable Brokerage Account.

a. Sell $2,000 worth of stocks every month in your **SEP-IRA**. If the **Bid** (the price you can sell at) of *ITOT*, *VT*, or *SPY* is $66.99 per share, sell 30 shares using a **Market Order** (make sure the U.S. stock market is open, avoid trading during the first and last half hour, and triple-check to make sure it's a **Sell** order and NOT a Buy order) to free up $2,000. Thanks to Fidelity, you might get a better price than what's shown—$66.995 for example.

b. Check your **Cash Available to Trade** in your **SEP-IRA**. If you have $5,010 ($2,000 from the sale of stocks, $3,000 from new savings, and a $10 residual balance) and the **Ask** (the price you can buy at) of *AGG*, *VMBS*, or *BIL* is $133.00 per share, buy 37 shares (always round down when buying) using a **Market Order** (triple-check to make sure it's a **Buy** order and NOT a Sell order). Thanks to Fidelity, you might get a better price than what's shown—$132.995 for example.

c. Check your **Cash Available to Trade** in your **Brokerage Account**. If you have $2,005 ($2,000 from new savings and a $5 residual balance) and the **Ask** (the price you can buy at) of ***ITOT***, ***VT***, or ***SPY*** is $67.00 per share, buy 29 shares (always round down when buying) using a **Market Order** (triple-check to make sure it's a **Buy** order and NOT a Sell order). Thanks to Fidelity, you might get a better price than what's shown—$66.995 for example.

d. If your IRAs become filled with bonds, you could repeat this process for your 401(k) by reallocating some of your current balance from stocks to bonds.

e. If your IRAs and 401(k) become filled with bonds, start buying bonds in your taxable Brokerage Account.

5. Wait two trading days for the money to officially settle. Log in to Fidelity.com, select your **SEP-IRA** (do this for your **Roth IRA** later), click the **Account Features** tab, click **Brokerage & Trading** to expand a menu of options, and click **Dividends and Capital**

Gains. The full name of your bond index fund will be listed here. Click the **Update** link at the end of that row. For **Dividends** and **Capital Gains**, click the options under **Reinvest in Security**. Also check the two boxes underneath so that any payments (interest, dividends, and capital gains) from your current and future investments are automatically reinvested.

6. You'll eventually have 60% of your money in stocks and 40% in bonds. This is a well-balanced investment *portfolio*. It's **medium-risk** instead of high-risk, and you might lose 18% in a very bad year instead of 30%, thus avoiding frequent 20% drawdowns. You'll earn **4–5% per year** in the long run instead of 5–6%.

7. **Rebalancing.** You'll rebalance once per year immediately after you file your taxes. First send your excess money to your SEP-IRA and Brokerage Account. Then figure out how much money you have in stocks and bonds. If stocks are LESS THAN 60% of your portfolio, you need to rebalance.

    a. In your IRAs, sell bonds (AGG, VMBS, or BIL) and buy stocks (ITOT, VT, or SPY) to get your portfolio back up to exactly 60% in stocks. For example, if you have $500,000 in stocks and $500,000 in bonds, sell $100,000 in bonds and buy $100,000 in stocks.

b. If your IRAs become filled with stocks, you can reallocate some of your current 401(k) balance from bonds to stocks.

c. If your IRAs and 401(k) become filled with stocks, don't sell bonds to buy stocks in your Brokerage Account. You'll owe taxes. Use your monthly savings to buy stocks until your portfolio is back up to 60% in stocks. Then switch back to buying bonds.

8. If you're still employed, rollover your 401(k) into your SEP-IRA when you leave your employer. You'll transfer it all over in cash, but leave your stock and bond allocations as they were. For example, if you had $80,000 in a total U.S. stock market index fund and $20,000 in an aggregate U.S. bond index fund in your 401(k), you'll buy $80,000 in stocks (ITOT, VT, or SPY) and $20,000 in bonds (AGG, VMBS, or BIL) in your SEP-IRA.

9. If you're more risk-tolerant than others, you should stick with a 60/40 portfolio for the rest of your life. You'll want to rebalance to exactly 60% in stocks and 40% in bonds every year once you're in or near (10 years away from) retirement.

10. Don't ever sell bonds to shift your portfolio back up to more than 60% in stocks. Once you're in a medium-risk plan, you'll stay in a medium- or low-risk plan forever. Going back to a high-risk plan would make you guilty of trying to time the market and ultimately cost you money.

INTERMEDIATE 30/70 PLAN

1. The 60/40 portfolio might be too risky for some retired people. Use the last 30 years of investing as your barometer—how well could you handle a market crash? There's no shame in being conservative, but you still need to face your fears with *minimal participation* in the stock market.

2. If you're near (10 years away from) retirement, rebalance to exactly 60% in stocks and 40% in bonds

every year if stocks are MORE THAN 60% of your portfolio. We'll let stocks slide down to 30%.

3. Sell stocks when you need to withdraw money in retirement.

4. You'll eventually have 30% of your money in stocks and 70% in bonds. Rebalance to exactly 30% in stocks and 70% in bonds every year.

5. 30/70 is a **low-risk** portfolio, and you might lose 9% in a very bad year instead of 30% or 18%, thus avoiding frequent 10% drawdowns. You'll earn **3–4% per year** in the long run.

6. Don't ever sell bonds to shift your portfolio back up to more than 30% in stocks. Once you're in a low-risk plan, you'll stay there forever. Going back to a high- or medium-risk plan would make you guilty of trying to time the market and ultimately cost you money.

5 | ADVANCED CONCEPTS

Skip the next two chapters if you're a finance newbie. They won't make sense until you've managed your own portfolio for five years or thoroughly gotten your ass kicked in a fun money trading account.

PERFORMANCE METRICS

EV, or expected value, is the sexiest two-letter combination for poker players (we live in an insular world…). When something is +EV, it has a positive **expected return**. Stocks have the highest expected return at 5.5% per year, then bonds at 2%, then cash at 1%. Poker players can be reckless cowboys though because we often ignore risk to capture that +EV.

I borrowed millions of dollars at 1–5% interest per year (including equity loans against my Corvette and my parents' house) to make 2–6% in the markets. 1% is still +EV, right? I didn't care that I could lose 80–100% in a market crash because my *identity* took precedence over my livelihood. My first downswing crushed me, and I had to grind low-stakes poker for a couple of years to get out of trouble. *When Genius Failed* is a great finance book that illustrates exactly this—smart people flying too close to the sun and getting burned.

Risk in the markets is measured by **volatility** (or **standard deviation**), which is how much an investment fluctuates. If the stock market has annualized volatility of 22%, it'll return somewhere between a 16.5% loss (5.5% − 22%) and 27.5% gain (5.5% + 22%) most years assuming a *normal distribution*. [Markets aren't always normal though, and they're prone to occasional periods of *reflexivity* where buying induces more buying or selling induces more selling. These self-reinforcing feedback loops create bubbles (too much buying) and crashes (too much selling).]

Traders measure the attractiveness of an investment by using both risk and return to calculate its **Sharpe ratio**—

(Expected Return − Cash Return) ÷ Volatility

Stocks have a Sharpe ratio of—

(5.5% − 1%) ÷ 22% = 0.2

With volatility of 5%, bonds have a Sharpe ratio of—

(2% − 1%) ÷ 5% = 0.2

The risk of stocks and bonds offset each other a little bit in a well-balanced portfolio. With volatility of 7.5%, the Sharpe ratio of 30% in stocks and 70% in bonds is roughly—

(30% × 5.5% + 70% × 2% − 1%) ÷ 7.5% = 0.27

This is better than stocks and bonds on their own and an effortless way to beat the market!

Not all investors look at risk the same way though, and someone who's young and wants to make a lot of money would be unsatisfied with a 30/70 portfolio. The Utility score (I call it the **Satisfaction score** because I'm not an economist with severe Asperger's) calculates how happy you might be with an investment—

Expected Return − ½ × Risk Aversion × Volatility^2

Risk Aversion is an assigned number that can range from 1.0 for an aggressive investor to 4.0 for an extremely conservative investor. The higher your Risk Aversion (the lower your risk tolerance), the more you penalize yourself per unit of risk. I've optimized the high-risk Basic Plan and medium-risk and low-risk Intermediate Plans so you can achieve the highest Satisfaction scores with minimal effort.

Younger investors (18–40) don't have much money and tend to be aggressive (Risk Aversion of 1.0). They should increase their savings rate to 25–50% (before taxes), and they'll have the highest Satisfaction score with 100% in stocks for maximum **Growth** until their replenish rate dips below 10%.

Middle-aged investors (40–65) have matured and developed good money habits, and they should have $500,000+. With a replenish rate below 10%, they won't recover as quickly from a market crash with new savings. They still want to grow their portfolios, but they're less aggressive now (Risk Aversion of 2.0). They'll have the highest Satisfaction score if they buy bonds for **Protection** and eventually get to 60% in stocks and 40% in bonds.

Retired investors (65+) who draw on $2,000,000+ in savings would be devastated by a market crash if they were fully invested in stocks. **Preservation** is more important than growth, but their conservativeness can vary widely (Risk Aversion between 2.0 and 4.0). Some will have the highest Satisfaction score if they stay with 60% in stocks and 40% in bonds, while others will be happiest with 30% in stocks and 70% in bonds.

ALPHA AND BETA

Beta is an estimate of your portfolio's sensitivity to the stock market, and it's an important measure of risk. A beta of 1.0 means that a 1% gain in the market normally leads to a 1% gain in your portfolio. A beta of 0.5 means that a 1% gain in the market normally leads to a 0.5% gain in your portfolio. A beta of 0 means that your portfolio normally has no relationship to the market. [Remember that markets aren't always normal.]

Alpha is an estimate of how much your portfolio outperforms the stock market based on its beta. If you're fully invested in the S&P 500 index (SPY) or Treasury bills (BIL), your alpha is exactly 0% per year (you neither outperform nor underperform the market). If you invest in the total U.S. stock market (ITOT) or the global stock market (VT), you pick up a tiny bit of alpha (0.05% for ITOT, 0.25% for VT). If you have a good mix of stocks and bonds (60/40 gets you to 0.6 beta, 30/70 gets you to 0.3 beta), you pick up a little more alpha (**0.5%**).

For comparison, investment professionals have long-term alphas in the range of −5% and +5% per year, and the average (after fees) is −2% or worse (i.e. most financial advisors, traders, and hedge funds don't beat the market). The average investor is closer to −5%. If you day trade or dick around with derivatives, you're worse than sheep—you're cannon fodder. Your alpha is -20% until you learn your lesson, and brokers, high-speed traders, banks, hedge funds, and trading exchanges feast on your mistakes.

TAX ALPHA

I've mentioned a few ways you can capture "tax alpha"—maximize contributions to your 401(k) and IRAs, put bonds in those tax-sheltered accounts and stocks in your Brokerage Account, and keep your money in your investment accounts for as long as possible.

Every dollar you don't pay to the IRS right away is a dollar you get to use interest-free for many years. If long-term interest rates are 1–2%, you'll pick up 1–2% for free EVERY YEAR by deferring taxes.

When we set the Cost Basis Information Tracking of our Fidelity taxable Brokerage Account to **Tax-Sensitive** (or **Maximize Short-Term Loss** with another brokerage), they make best efforts to minimize your tax impact. You could try choosing **Specific Shares** to sell for *tax-loss harvesting* (intentionally selling at a loss to reduce taxes at the end of the year). Work around the *wash sale rule* (you lose the tax benefit if you buy the same ETF within 30 days) by replacing an ETF that you sell with a different one (e.g. selling ITOT and replacing it with VT or SPY for stocks, selling AGG and replacing it with VMBS or BIL for bonds).

You'd better know what you're doing though because it's easy to muck up. I've made huge tax mistakes in my Brokerage Account. I was pissed off on January 2, 2020, when I sold an ETF one month before it would've qualified for a lower tax rate. This could've been a $1,000 gift for Uncle Sam, but the coronavirus crash allowed me to harvest losses against that gain.

TRADING

There's a well-known quote that opens the poker movie *Rounders*: "If you can't spot the sucker in your first half hour at the table, then you are the sucker." In finance, almost everyone's a sucker, and the biggest suckers are the ones who trade often and try the hardest.

How do you spot these fish in public? Look for puffery—people who eagerly talk about all the money they made. They don't have verifiable track records, but somehow they had perfect foresight when it came to bitcoin, Tesla, put options in a falling market, or whatever facet of finance they feel like chirping about that week. Anyone can claim to have a 12-inch dick when they wear jeans that are too big (I say this as someone who was also filled with piss and vinegar). As Denzel Washington says in *American Gangster*, "The loudest one in the room is the weakest one in the room."

What's the reward for being a glorified day trader? If you're good at picking stocks without inside information, you might be able to beat the market by 0.1% per year. If you can use fundamentals (news) or technicals (silly charts) to time bitcoin or other commodities better than professional traders, you might be able to beat the market by 0.1% per year.

Actually, you won't gain an edge from "fundamentals" or "technicals" at all. As my friend Ken says, this dichotomy is just a commercial narrative meant to induce the CNBC-watching public to trade often and lose lots of money. The goal of media has always been to incite fear and anxiety so they can sell you an expensive solution from their sponsors.

Also, prices move first; fundamentals come AFTER prices have already moved. You will NEVER be able to get in front of it. Stocks crashed long before ANYONE predicted the rapid spread of the 2020 coronavirus across the U.S.

If you learn a basic time-series momentum (trend-following) strategy and have the emotional fortitude to execute it with perfect discipline across stock and bond indexes, currencies, and commodities, you might be able to beat the market by 1% per year. I wasted a year of my life building my own version of this trade before I realized there was already an ETF for it (WTMF). And while it *theoretically* produces massive risk-adjusted returns when you run simulations on historical data, I doubt it has a 1% edge anymore in the real world.

At the beginning of your journey with the odds stacked heavily against you, you'll be optimistic and overconfident, and you'll underperform the market by 20% per year. If you work hard and spend 1,000 hours per year for 10 years on stock picking and market timing with a good feedback system, on a $1 million portfolio, you'll make an extra $1,000–10,000 per year (**$1–10 per hour**) for your day trading efforts.

An alternate route is to get PhDs in particle physics and computational neuroscience at an Ivy League school. Then you can sell your soul to finance and its cutthroat culture—maybe work at a hedge fund. You'll have to abstain from a social life for 10 years if you want to make partner as a head trader or portfolio manager. Good luck!

MARKET TIMING REVISITED

I get a concerned text message every year from every friend and relative about the stock market (one friend in particular freaks out every few months). The narrative is the same EVERY SINGLE TIME. The stock market pushes to all-time highs as it's done for the last seven years (new highs create **attachment**, and attachment creates anxiety and fear of loss). Then it dips 10%. Then they panic and ask if it's time to get out of stocks.

For the last 100 years, the market has fallen at least 10% from its peak 7 out of every 10 years. The average drawdown within any calendar year is 17%. Why is THIS the year—ON A 10% DIP—when finance falls apart?

In big poker games in Los Angeles, I would salivate whenever a weak player sat down at my table with thousands of dollars. These whales would inevitably lose all their money, and sometimes a professional poker player would replace them. I would then panic, especially if I was winning (never count your money when you're sitting at the table, and never look at your financial statements more than once per year).

I would get in my head, telling myself that a $100 per hour game turned into a $50 per hour game. And I didn't quit my $100,000 per year job to make a paltry $50 per hour. So I would leave early, working only a few hours instead of a full day.

I was rationalizing my **FEAR**. None of the other pros were skilled enough to make a dent in my win rate, and there was plenty of easy money at the table. I should've been making $50–100 per hour for 1,500–2,000 hours every year. Instead of leaning into my discomforts and **staying in the game all the time**, I let my fears consume me. I failed at a career in poker because I gave up too easily.

People thought the market topped out when the S&P 500 index crossed the 2,000 mark in 2014. Yet here we are six years later and that index is higher now, even after the coronavirus crash. I've been buying at market highs every year and helping friends and family do the same, and we've made a lot of money while others live in fear.

You can wait for the stars to align perfectly. Or you can **stay in the game all the time** and put your cash to work RIGHT NOW. Not tomorrow, not in an hour—literally RIGHT NOW!

The problem with trying to time the market is that you will NEVER find a "good" entry point. Any faulty logic you tell yourself will ALWAYS be a *rationalization* for an emotional decision. What if the market falls another 30%? What if the global economy collapses? What if the S&P 500 index never tops 3,000 again? What if, what if, what if—where does the cognitive entropy end!

It ends by tuning out all of the bullshit. Wherever the stock market is at today, IT DOESN'T MATTER. If your name is George Soros, you can try to time the market. Everyone else—have a long-term investment plan and deliberately stick to it.

MEAN REVERSION

You probably have no idea what mean reversion means. If you flip a coin six times and it comes up tails every time, is it more likely to come up heads or tails the next time? It's even—50/50. If a roulette wheel lands on black six times, is it more likely to land on red or black the next time? It's even—47.4/47.4 (2.6% for each of the green zeros).

Let's say intelligence is rated on a 1–10 scale. If I'm a 10 and my partner's a 9, our children wouldn't "mean revert" to be **absolutely** dumb 3–5s. They'd inherit our intelligence and maybe be 6–8s. This would make them

relatively dumb compared to their outlier parents but smart compared to their average peers in a public school.

Conversely, if two repulsive 3s hooked up inside portable toilets at a state fair, they might have some slightly ugly or average-looking kids. They won't have any super attractive ones though unless they pop out dozens of kids (they can't ALL be ugly).

The stock market return over the last 100 years has been incredible. We've had a lot of +20% and +30% years from 2009 to 2019 too. Did this mean we were in a bubble and "due" for a coronavirus correction? Could you or anyone else predict that a fish market in Wuhan, China would initiate a pandemic or that Russia would start a price war with the OPEC oil cartel?

Maybe we were never in a bubble. Maybe low-cost ETFs have allowed investors to evolve, which takes easy money out of the game. Professional poker players made $100 per hour 15 years ago without a sweat. Now they have to work hard to crack $50 per hour in a market that's *matured*.

We won't make 7–9% per year in the stock market anymore. Maybe prices are as they should be—not inflated—and 5–6% is the **new normal**. If you're sitting on cash and waiting for old normal opportunities to mean revert, be prepared to wait a lifetime while everyone else makes money. [By the way, right now during the 2020 coronavirus recovery is your opportunity to earn 7% per year.]

THE LIQUIDITY RISK PREMIUM

Monday, August 24, 2015 was a day that seared into my mind forever. I rolled out of bed at 8 a.m. CST and turned on all my trading screens. The stock market opened at a reasonable price, but within minutes it took a nosedive and fell 5%. I was invested in non-index ETFs at the time that weren't very *liquid* (I use ONLY index ETFs now), and because a fair price couldn't be established for these ETFs, my trading software was showing a loss of 25%.

The best thing you can do in a **liquidity crisis** is to recognize that these prices aren't real. You sit on your hands and wait for the storm to pass. That's what I did. It took an hour for traders to establish legitimate prices, and every minute of that hour was nauseating.

I had borrowed on margin from my broker (this means using your investments as collateral for a cash loan) to invest 600% of my money across stocks, bonds, credit, currencies, and gold. I came dangerously close to a margin call—if you trade on margin and lose too much money, your broker will start liquidating your investments. They won't hesitate to sell at unreasonable prices in a liquidity panic, which would destroy you.

The storm passed and markets recovered half their losses by the end of the week. Every liquidity crisis is the same. A catalyst causes the stock market to fall precipitously. Then the weak players all run for the exit at the same time. This occasionally makes every asset class lose—diversification is no boon in a liquidity crisis. Eventually buyers come in once the weak players are shaken out, and the market makes a sharp recovery halfway from its low point.

Why not try to buy at the bottom? Because you'll have no idea if it takes 15 minutes, 15 days, or 15 months to shake out all the weak players. And when you try to pick bottoms, you get sticky fingers.

Continue buying stocks or bonds with your new savings every month during these periods of stress. Other than that, sit on your hands and DO NOTHING. Whatever happens, happens, and sometimes nothing is the hardest thing to do.

Liquidity is a measure of how easy it is to trade say $1 million without changing the price. Large U.S. stocks and the nine ETFs used in this book have maximum liquidity, so you don't have to worry about losing 25% when the market is down 5%.

International and small U.S. stocks are far less liquid. They lose more money in a crisis (because there isn't a market to liquidate them), and they have a **liquidity risk premium** to compensate that extra risk. An interest rate of 1–2%, plus an equity risk premium of 4%, plus a liquidity risk premium of 1–3% equals a 6–9% return for less liquid investments. It's closer to 6% for international and small U.S. stock index ETFs. It's closer to 9% for private equity (investing in small, private companies) before outrageous management fees.

I prefer the global stock market (VT) and the total U.S. stock market (ITOT) over the S&P 500 index (SPY). Through these funds, you can capture some of the liquidity risk premium as long as you're not a weak player who panics during a crisis.

ECONOMIC SEASONS

Experienced investment professionals are mindful of the four different economic "seasons"—

- Strong growth, high inflation
  (Stocks outperform)

- Strong growth, low inflation
  (Stocks and bonds rise)

- Weak growth, low inflation
  (Bonds outperform)

- Weak growth, high inflation
  (Stocks and bonds fall)

Stocks perform well in two out of four seasons—let's call them spring and summer. Investing in stocks and bonds allows you to thrive in three out of four seasons—spring, summer, and autumn—but you won't fare well during periods of high inflation and weak growth.

In winter, as we saw with the inflation scare in February 2017, we all suffer. Instead of investing in just stocks and bonds, we could add the U.S. Dollar index and gold. This offers some protection against long and cold winters.

Normally with insurance, you pay money to protect yourself when accidents result in a broken leg, a burned-down house, or a wrecked car. But with bonds, U.S. Dollar index, and gold, which are considered hedges (partial insurance) against a falling stock market, it's like you're GETTING PAID to insure yourself, even when accidents don't happen! This isn't a guarantee, and all of these assets can tank in a liquidity crisis. A multi-asset portfolio withstands the winter though, and you can reap most of the rewards of the stock market with far less risk.

6 | ADVANCED PLANS

You need to be retired with at least $2 million to make a Multi-Asset Plan worth your time. You can get started on an Advanced 60/40 Plan with only $250,000.

The Multi-Asset Plan detailed in this chapter is more than a little complicated. If you haven't yet mastered a 60/40 or 30/70 portfolio of stocks and bonds, it'll be impossible to manage a 4-asset portfolio without making mistakes. Most people should stick with the Basic and Intermediate Plans.

If you want more protection across the economic seasons and don't mind some extra work, a multi-asset strategy is perfect. Stocks make money, bonds make money, and stocks and bonds have a negative correlation. We just need a couple of other money-making assets that have a low correlation to stocks and bonds.

LONG-TERM TREASURIES

When the Federal Reserve adjusts interest rates, the effect is much stronger on long-term bonds than short-term bonds. Let's say you receive an IOU for loaning a friend $100,000 to buy a house at an interest rate of 3% per year for 30 years (we'll assume he never defaults). He'll owe you $422 per month for 360 months. If the market interest rate goes up to 4% immediately after you give him money, the IOU is worth way less—$88,000 instead of $100,000—because you could write the same IOU and receive $477 per month instead of $422. If the market interest rate drops to 2%, the IOU is worth way more—$114,000 instead of $100,000—because you're receiving $422 per month instead of $370.

Long-term Treasury bonds (10- to 30-year bonds issued by the U.S. government) currently (but not always and not forever) have a negative correlation with the stock market. This means they like to go up when stocks go down, and they also like to go down when stocks go up—their risks partially offset each other. They're risky though, and it's not uncommon to lose a lot of money in both stocks and long-term Treasuries.

Spreading your money across 2 risky stocks is safer than 1 risky stock, and 500 risky stocks are safer than 2 risky stocks. Spreading your money across 2 risky assets—stocks and long-term Treasuries—is [much] safer than putting all of it in the stock market. A long-term Treasury bond index fund (**TLT**) earns roughly 1% more per year than short-term Treasury bills.

CURRENCIES

Before the 2008 financial crisis, currencies were a great way to pick up interest. You could deposit U.S. Dollars into an online savings account and earn 5% for doing nothing and risking nothing! Higher inflation eroded a lot of the gains, but those were great times to be lazy.

Cash in the bank doesn't earn anything anymore, and you have to invest your hard-earned U.S. Dollars in Treasury bills (BIL) if you want more than 0.1% interest. What if currency investing wasn't limited to U.S. Dollars? What if you could borrow money from countries with low interest rates and use that money to invest in currencies with higher interest rates?

Welcome to the Currency Carry Trade. The U.S. Dollar currently has an interest rate of +0.25%, while the Euro has an interest rate of −0.75%. You're paid the difference of +1% to borrow Euros and invest in U.S. Dollars. This spread opens to 1–2% in the long run. Before the 2020 coronavirus, it was 2–3%!

This trade is risky though because it's sensitive to exchange rate changes between the U.S. Dollar and the Euro. If the U.S. Dollar appreciates (strengthens), you'll need less U.S. Dollars to pay back your Euro loan. You've made additional money on this trade because you get to pocket the extra U.S. Dollars. If the U.S. Dollar depreciates (weakens), you'll need more U.S. Dollars to pay back your Euro loan, and so you've lost money. The risk of major currencies is lower than stocks and long-term Treasuries.

Purchasing Power Parity is an economic theory that says the exchange rate between two countries should be proportional to the price of goods in both locations. For example, if a Big Mac (or diversified basket of goods) sells for $5 in the U.S. and 5 Euros in Europe, then the exchange rate should gravitate toward 1.00 U.S. Dollar per Euro. If an iPad (or diversified basket of goods) sells for $500 in the U.S. and 50,000 Yen in Japan, then the exchange rate should gravitate toward 100 Yen per U.S. Dollar.

There's some validity to Purchasing Power Parity, and sophisticated trading models also adjust for differences in economic output and inflation. It takes a long time for parity to come to fruition though. For simplification, we'll ignore fancy economic theories like Purchasing Power Parity and just look at interest rates.

When I worked in oil trading, we would calculate the price of heavy fuel oil in our U.S. storage tanks, the price the Chinese were willing to pay, and the cost of shipping that oil on very large tankers from the U.S. to China. If that trade was profitable, we would say, "The Arb is open!" *Arbitrage* is pompous trader-speak for an abnormal opportunity to profit at low risk. Arbitrage isn't always low-risk though—traders are often book-smart and street-dumb, and many hedge funds have collapsed because of academic hubris.

Currency Carry isn't arbitrage per se, but it's still a profitable trade that anyone can do from home. We'll invest in the U.S. Dollar index fund (**UUP**). This fund is "long" U.S. dollars and "short" mostly Euros plus a few other currencies. It won't make as much as stocks, but it can make as much as bonds when the carry is *open*.

In addition to the 1–2% long-term difference between U.S. Dollars and Euros, you'll pick up another 1–2% from regular U.S. interest. When you invest money in UUP, all of it is converted to short-term Treasury bills as collateral. If the U.S. Dollar depreciates, some of that collateral is used to repay your loans in other currencies that have appreciated against the U.S. Dollar.

You don't actually borrow cash Euros from European banks and deposit cash U.S. Dollars in American banks—that's cost-intensive. Instead, UUP buys U.S. Dollar index futures contracts. This is like a cost-efficient wager between two people on the future price of the U.S. Dollar index, and full payment is guaranteed by the ICE trading exchange.

UUP pairs especially well with the global stock market index fund (VT). Foreign companies sell goods in foreign currencies (duh!), and UUP hedges that money—which is eventually exchanged into U.S. Dollars for American investors—against a weakening U.S. Dollar.

With fees of 0.79% per year, UUP is a very expensive fund. By signing up for Fidelity's Fully Paid Lending Program, your shares of UUP are loaned out to traders who arbitrage this expensive fund with cheaper alternatives. The interest you'll pick up mitigates most of the 0.79%. To be clear, you'll still own these shares and any profits and losses until you sell them.

GOLD AND OTHER COMMODITIES

Commodities are TERRIBLE investments. Most commodities, like food and energy, are meant to be consumed. If you think crude oil is a good investment, load your garage with barrels of it for 10 years and see if it was worth the trouble.

All money made from commodities is in the operations, logistics, and price discrepancies. In other words, TRADING, not investing. If you worked at a big oil company, you could ship heavy fuel oil from refineries in Europe over to the U.S. Then you could blend that dirty oil with diesel to make *barely legal* marine fuel for cruise ships and container ships. The big oil company would make millions of dollars every year, of which you'd get a tiny cut.

We are not traders, nor should we ever aspire to be. Regardless of what you hear on CNBC or from a financial advisor, commodities are not a legitimate investment. We can make an exception for gold and silver because they're currencies.

Gold and silver coins were legal tender long before paper money existed. You could buy a nice suit with an ounce of gold 100 years ago. If your great-grandfather had stored an ounce of gold for you in a safe deposit box, you could buy a nice suit with an ounce of gold today. Had he instead put $25 cash (the price of a suit back then) into a safe deposit box, you couldn't buy a nice $1,500 suit today. And yet people still keep large cash balances in zero-interest bank accounts.

Silver isn't a terrible investment. I don't care for it though because it's expensive to store and insure. It also has some positive correlation with the stock market.

Gold is a great investment in small doses though—specifically 5–10% of your portfolio. Let's say you buy it for $1,500 per ounce this year (2020), store and insure it for $1.50 per year, then lock into a futures contract to sell it for $1,516.50 next year. That's a 1% risk-free return, which is higher than this year's interest rate of 0.1%.

We're don't want to sell it in one year though. We want to hold it as a long-term investment. That comes with risk, and the price of gold is just as risky as the stock market.

Like bonds, many people consider gold to be a "flight to safety," where its price tends to go up when the stock market or economy goes down. Others think it's a hedge against inflation. Whether you look at 10 years or 100 years of data, you'll see that gold has zero correlation to economic growth and zero correlation to inflation.

It's not insurance, but you still earn more than short-term Treasury bills for something that has zero correlation to stocks. Gold is therefore another source of alpha. It's even better when you pair it with the Currency Carry Trade because gold has a negative correlation to the U.S. Dollar.

We won't buy physical gold on our own (high transaction cost) to put in a safe deposit box (high storage and insurance cost). Instead, we'll invest in a gold trust fund (**IAU**) that buys, stores, and insures physical gold for you at minimal cost.

CHOICE

Your choice is between the intermediate plans in Chapter 4 and these advanced plans. If it's hard to decide right now, just stick with the intermediate plans because they're much easier.

We'll use long-term Treasuries (TLT) in the Advanced 60/40 Plan. Then we'll add the other alternative investments, U.S. Dollar index (UUP) and gold (IAU), to the Multi-Asset Plan.

ADVANCED 60/40 PLAN

1. Instead of aggregate bonds (AGG), mortgage-backed securities (VMBS), and Treasury bills (BIL), we'll invest in long-term Treasury bonds (TLT). Do everything the same as the Intermediate 60/40 Plan, buying ***TLT*** until you get to exactly 60% in stocks and 40% in bonds.

    a. The one difference is that your 401(k) contributions will continue to go to stocks. However much in new savings is going to your 401(k) each month, sell that amount in stocks (ITOT, VT, or SPY) and buy TLT in your IRAs.

    b. If your IRAs become filled with TLT, you can reallocate some of your 401(k) from stocks to the aggregate U.S. bond index fund until you get to 40% in bonds. It's not as good as TLT, but it's better than buying bonds in your taxable Brokerage Account.

    c. If your IRAs and 401(k) become filled with bonds, buy TLT in your Brokerage Account until you get to 40% in bonds.

2. **Rebalancing.** TLT is a poor investment on its own or in extremely large doses. To maintain a balanced portfolio, allocate new savings to the underperforming asset class every month. If you don't have 35–45% in bonds (this is known as 10% *slippage*), rebalance to exactly 60% in stocks and 40% in bonds. Try to avoid selling anything in your taxable Brokerage Account, but don't let TLT build up to over 50% of your portfolio either.

3. This is a **medium-risk** strategy, just like the Intermediate 60/40 Plan. Alpha improves from 0.5% to **1%**.

MULTI-ASSET PLAN

1. Ignore this plan if your Brokerage Account holds much more than 30% of your savings and you have a lot of taxable gains. Go back to the Intermediate 30/70 Plan if you want to lower your risk. This advanced strategy isn't worth paying taxes early.

2. Let's make sure the Currency Carry Trade is wide open. Go to **WorldGovernmentBonds.com** and open the **United States** in one tab and **Germany** in

another. Look for the **1 year** rates. Subtract Germany's rate from the United States'. If it's less than **+0.5%**, go back to the Intermediate 30/70 Plan.

3. To keep it simple, we'll compartmentalize your 401(k) as a distinct strategy from the Multi-Asset Plan.

   a. Reallocate 30% of the current balance and future contributions to a stock index fund and 70% to a bond index fund.

   b. Enable automatic rebalances—quarterly if they'll allow it. Otherwise, annually is fine.

   c. Set up automatic RMD withdrawals when you're 72 years old. You'll never have to look at your 401(k) again!

4. We'll invest 40% of your money in the U.S. Dollar index (UUP), 30% in stocks (preferably VT, but ITOT and SPY can also work), 20% in long-term Treasuries (TLT), and 10% in gold (IAU). Even though it seems like the U.S. Dollar index allocation is huge, remember that currencies are less risky than stocks, long-term Treasuries, and gold. Half your risk

is still in stocks, some is in bonds, some is in the Currency Carry Trade, and a small amount is in gold.

5. Trade within your IRAs first, then in your taxable Brokerage Account if necessary. Get your portfolio to 40% **UUP**, 30% **VT**, 20% **TLT**, and 10% **IAU**. Ideally, all the money in your Brokerage Account should be in stocks. Avoid buying UUP in your Brokerage Account because you'll receive a Schedule K–1 tax form that's a MASSIVE pain to file correctly.

6. **Advanced Rebalancing.** [Turn off automatic reinvestment of dividends and capital gains to make this a little easier.] To maintain a balanced portfolio, allocate new savings every month to get within 36–44% for **UUP**, 27–33% for **VT**, 18–22% for **TLT**, and 9–11% for **IAU** (this is known as 10% *slippage*). Rebalance if you need to. Rebalancing a 4-asset portfolio sucks ass, so go back to the Intermediate 30/70 Plan if you want simplicity.

7. **Currency Carry Check.** Once per year, go to **WorldGovernmentBonds.com** and open the **United States** in one tab and **Germany** in another. Look for

the **1 year** rates. If the United States' rate is below Germany's, then the Currency Carry Trade is closed.

   a. The way things look right now, this Currency Carry Trade should stay open for the next 30 years. But the world can change from one year to the next, so it's important to make sure the U.S. Dollar interest rate is higher than the Euro (or Germany's) interest rate every year.

   b. If the Currency Carry Trade closes, switch to the Intermediate 30/70 Plan. Feel free to keep gold (IAU) in case the Currency Carry Trade reopens.

8. This is a **low-risk** strategy, just like the Intermediate 30/70 Plan. Alpha improves from 0.5% to **1%**.

7 | ADDITIONAL TOPICS

Skip the first three sections of this chapter if you're a finance newbie. Continue with the Basic Estate Planning section.

THE BIG CARRY

I use an extension of the Multi-Asset Plan for my personal investing accounts and helping friends and family with theirs. My advanced model is called *The Big Carry*, and it gets its name from various **carry trades**.

When a normal Treasury curve (when the 30-year rate is higher than the 5-year rate) stays the same from one year to the next, you pick up 0.5–1% *roll-down carry* with long-term Treasuries. When foreign exchange rates stay the same from one year to the next, you pick up 1–2% *currency carry* by borrowing Euros to buy U.S. Dollars. When credit ratings stay the same for high-risk (speculative grade) governments and corporations from one year to the next, you pick up 2–3% *credit carry*. These carries are added to the regular interest rate.

The coronavirus and subsequent oil price collapse induced a liquidity crisis in March 2020, and I got smoked from credit investments (credit carry goes up the stairs and down the elevator). Their risk and return are the same as stocks during this recovery, so I'd rather **keep it simple** and hold stocks instead.

Just like the Multi-Asset Plan, we're currently invested in global stock indexes, long-term Treasuries, U.S. Dollar against just Euro (instead of the whole U.S. Dollar index), and Japanese Yen against U.S. Dollar (Yen functions similarly to gold). We then apply leverage.

LEVERAGE

If you invest in all of these carry trades directly by financing 100% of each position with cash, you'll have a very low-risk portfolio with low returns (it still crushes cash). Futures, forwards, and swaps (fancy derivatives) are used to **leverage** investments to 150–250% and create a bespoke high-, medium-, or low-risk solution for each individual's portfolio. Our risk is lower than the stock market even though 150–250% sounds insane!

Financial alchemy is incredibly dangerous if you don't know what you're doing. And when you play the game of leverage, you win or you die (most people die). Each component is extremely volatile and a poor investment on its own (derivatives have significantly negative Satisfaction scores). Used in small and measured proportions, they can be combined to create something beautiful (the highest Satisfaction score for each portfolio).

Leverage and asset allocation (not random stock picking or market timing) are why hedge funds have alpha. Big asset management institutions like mutual funds and pensions don't use leverage, so they give the appearance of beating the market by investing in riskier *growth* stocks. Warren Buffett appears to be the best investor of all time because he invests 160% in *value* stocks that have better risk-adjusted returns (higher Sharpe ratios). His insurance business also allows him to borrow money at 0% (free alpha of 3–4% per year across his 50 years at Berkshire Hathaway).

Value stocks are just the tip of the iceberg. Lower-risk assets like credit, bonds, and currencies that investors avoid (because they can't or won't leverage) usually have the highest risk-adjusted returns. If you combine carry trades with stock and bond investments, then use leverage to scale up to a desired level of risk, you'll have an investment portfolio with very high alpha.

RESULTS

The Big Carry produces a theoretical alpha of **2–3%** per year using leveraged ETFs, and it's accessible to retail (non-professional) investors who really know what they're doing. Development of a full gamut of micro futures contracts (for investors with less than $10 million) would allow them to pick up another 1–2%. By expanding into low-cost private equity and picking up individual bonds instead of relying on stock and bond ETFs, *The Big Carry* would also capture more of the liquidity risk premium. The total alpha could be as high as 5–6%!

I'm happy to show you how it works. Actual results—my full track record—can be found at FinanceBro.net.

BASIC ESTATE PLANNING

Nobody wants to think about death. But if something should happen to you, 8% of your hard-earned savings will go to court, executor, attorney, accounting, and appraisal fees in probate—the long (1–2 years) judicial process where your assets, or estate, are distributed to your heirs.

One option for avoiding probate is to establish a *living trust*, which is also costly and time-consuming. A living trust is unnecessary if you take a few simple steps—

- *Joint Ownership*
  If you're married, make sure your homes, cars, bank accounts, and other valuable property are jointly owned.

- *IRA, 401(k), and Pension Accounts*
  Designate primary and secondary beneficiaries.

- *Brokerage Accounts*
  Designate primary and secondary beneficiaries with a transfer-on-death (TOD) form.

- *Bank Accounts*
  Add payable-on-death (POD) designations.

- *Homes*
  Sign transfer-on-death (TOD) deeds.

- *Cars*
  Name transfer-on-death (TOD) beneficiaries.

These assets will pass to your spouse or beneficiaries without having to go through probate. For *Personal Property*, if the value of your remaining estate (jewelry, art, furniture, etc.) is less than the minimum threshold in your state, they can opt for a simplified or summary probate—or sometimes skip probate entirely.

FINANCIAL ADVISORS

My mind runs like a Ferrari engine, and I have trouble slowing it down. I might need a therapist, but I don't have the patience to interview 20–30 of them to find a good one. Many therapists lack empathy and attack their patients. Many therapists have their own neuroses. Many therapists don't know what the hell they're talking about (including psychologists with PhDs).

I've been through a dozen therapists, and most are useless beyond basic life-coping skills. If you're generally healthy, you don't need a therapist. You just need to move your body, meditate, and make friends.

You also need to interview 20–30 investment professionals (not the client-facing salesmen) to find a good one. He needs to be trustworthy. He needs to clearly articulate why his investment process has a meaningful edge over low-cost index funds (his track record doesn't mean shit). His *management fee* needs to be less than 1% per year. [If he charges a *performance fee* that's based on investment gains, run away from him. I've seen traders cheat the system by negligently taking on excessive risk in losing years.]

You need to spread your money across several advisors too. Having one or two advisors is risky. If one makes a big mistake, he could cripple your wealth. You don't want more than four though—too many cooks can spoil the broth. Hopefully you have time to interview 100 investment professionals.

Implementation takes minimal effort. If you can't execute the basic or intermediate strategies in this book and you need someone to hold your hand for the rest of your life, maybe you should pay some asshole 1–2% ($1,000–2,000 per $100,000) per year in direct management fees and another 1–3% ($1,000–3,000 per $100,000) in hidden fees.

Hiring a financial advisor is like paying lots of money to go to college, but you don't get a fancy degree. Investing in low-cost index funds is like going to the library and getting that education for FREE.

ANNUITIES AND DEFINED BENEFIT PLANS

If the financial industry is hell, the insurance industry is its ninth circle, and it's filled with Judas salesmen. In the aftermath of the 2008 financial crisis, many retirees forfeited the entirety of their life savings to seek safety under the shelter of annuities. They did this without deconstructing complex actuarial tables that obfuscate how badly insurance companies rape us in the butt. To make that pain worse, they watched from the sidelines as the stock market roared to new highs over the next 10 years.

If stock market swings are too much for you to stomach in retirement, you should be in the low-risk Intermediate Plan that's 30% in stocks and 70% in bonds. This minimal participation allows you to face your fears with lots of stability. You would've lost 11% instead of 55% from the drawdown of October 9, 2007, to March 9, 2009. Then you would've made 150% (9.5% per year) over the next 10 years.

TARGET DATE FUNDS

I mentioned avoiding target date funds in the Basic Plan, and that's because they're scams. Admittedly, they have the huge benefit of automatically shifting your asset allocation from 90% in stocks and 10% in bonds right now to 60% in stocks and 40% in bonds in 30 years. But they use a wide range of unnecessary mutual funds (e.g. international bonds with negative interest rates). They also charge two layers of fees—0.5–1% ($500–1,000 per $100,000) per year for pooling these funds together and an additional 0.5–2% ($500–2,000 per $100,000) for the mutual funds.

ROBO-ADVISORS

The popular robo-advisors are legit. For just 0.25–0.5% ($250–500 per $100,000) per year, they'll also shift your asset allocation from 90% in stocks and 10% in bonds right now to 60% in stocks and 40% in bonds in 30 years. They use low-cost index ETFs instead of expensive mutual funds, but their range is also too wide and unnecessary (e.g. international bonds with negative interest rates, real estate, commodities). They also can't manage your 401(k), so you'll still have to spend time on asset allocation. For 15 minutes per year of minimal effort, I'd rather save 0.25% ($250 per $100,000) per year and have more control over my investments with the do-it-yourself Basic and Intermediate Plans.

REAL ESTATE

Most Americans are financially illiterate, and our favorite long-term savings vehicle is cash. Real estate is a close second, and stocks rank a distant third. Like I've said over and over, cash is TRASH. Real estate is sometimes just as bad.

Real estate could mean real estate investment trusts (REITs) and real estate index funds, and you already have these in your portfolio. Stock index funds invest across eleven different sectors of the economy, and real estate is one of them. Real estate is also highly correlated to financial services, which is the largest of these sectors along with technology.

If you invest in the NASDAQ-100 index instead of the S&P 500 index, you would be overly concentrated in technology and have a very poor portfolio. Investing in additional real estate funds will also unbalance your portfolio and lead to underperformance (even though this is EXACTLY what financial advisors do because "real estate" is a marketing gimmick that has mindless consumeristic appeal). Don't try to guess which sectors of the economy will outperform—just buy the total market (ITOT, VT, or SPY).

Real estate could also mean owning several individual properties and renting them out. They *can* be decent investments because of the 1–3% liquidity risk premium—the same premium you pick up by investing in various small or private businesses. You must be meticulous though.

Just like buying your own home, you have to negotiate well so you don't pay 20–30% above fair value. You can't pay ridiculous 7% fees to real estate agents either. You need to secure mortgages with interest rates below 3–3.5%. And you must rent out every single room year-round—avoid leaving it vacant most of the year as your vacation home. Any one of these mistakes turns a rental property into a very poor investment. If it's stressful to be someone's landlord or expensive to hire a management company, it's not worth it.

You shouldn't invest more than **10–30%** of your wealth across various rental properties. Follow that same **10–30%** rule for a portfolio of small or private businesses (assuming you're meticulous with them too). Most of your wealth should be in stocks (ITOT, VT, or SPY) and bonds (AGG, VMBS, or BIL). 98% of my wealth is in stocks, bonds, and currencies (245% with leverage, actually), and I don't feel like I'm missing out on much.

CRYPTOCURRENCIES

I wish I had a riding crop to smack people in the face every time they mention cryptocurrencies in an investment discussion. Let's just call it exactly what it is—GAMBLING, not investing. Cryptocurrencies have unfortunately become popular with the finance community, and they're here to stay. So now I have to waste a couple of pages of this book unpacking this horseshit.

I have a lot of friends in poker and tech, and many of them have massive amounts of their wealth in cryptocurrencies. I'm extremely judgmental if you couldn't tell, and I think they're all idiots (but I still love them).

Many argue that bitcoin (and other cryptocurrencies) have zero correlation with the stock market. That might be true in normal times, but it's more vulnerable to a liquidity crisis than other assets. When everyone panicked in March 2020 because of the coronavirus, bitcoin's beta skyrocketed to nearly 1.0. It lost just as much as the stock market on big down days, sometimes MUCH more (-37% on March 12).

Bitcoin and ether might eventually become legitimate currencies, but right now their primary use is speculative (I don't know anyone who actually pays for goods and services with them). How much of our portfolio should we allocate to a speculative currency like gold that *might* have alpha? 5–10%. Cryptocurrencies are 5–10 times more volatile than gold though, so you shouldn't invest (or gamble) more than **0.5–1%** in each one. Whenever you speculate (or gamble) on anything, you shouldn't risk more than 0.5–1% if you could lose a lot of money quickly.

AUTOMATIC ENROLLMENT

You should be set for life if you can create good habits and implement the Basic and Intermediate Plans in this book. But it's much harder than it sounds because you're going to RESIST making necessary changes in your life. Doing anything other than what your emotional status quo wants you to do is TOO HARD.

Financiers prey on our behavioral weaknesses. That's why we pay ridiculous fees to financial advisors, that's why we gamble and day trade, and that's why the average investor underperforms the market by 5% per year. Why does the financial industry exist at all? Because we're human, because we're emotional, and because we're impulsive and short-sighted. No child (or adult in my case) can wait 15 minutes for two chocolate chip cookies if there's one immediately available.

Richard Thaler, a behavioral economist at the University of Chicago, and Cass Sunstein proposed that governments *Nudge* us (but not force us) in a direction that's in our best interests. I think this is a great idea!

Employers could automatically enroll every employee in a 401(k) plan at the time they're hired, withhold 10% of every paycheck, and increase that 10% contribution by 1% every three months until you get to a 25% savings rate in four years. Your contributions would go into a total U.S. stock market index fund until you're 50 years old, then new contributions would go into an aggregate U.S. bond index fund. This would be the default option—you must OPT OUT if you'd rather spend 100% of your money and miss out on matching contributions.

You won't have a useless human resources manager nudging you in the right direction if you're self-employed. But you can follow those same guidelines (shoot for a 50% savings rate if possible!). If you're smart enough to run a business, you're smart enough to make automatic monthly contributions to your SEP-IRA and Brokerage Account.

CONCLUSION

I never really think about money anymore. I've lost hundreds of thousands of dollars from the 2020 coronavirus panic. I'll have to work twice as hard for 30% less income for the next few years too. But I'm not worried—not even a little bit. I understand that investing is a very long game, and you'll crush it if you follow a solid process and don't take on excessive risk.

Investing doesn't have to be overwhelming or time-consuming. You can apply the principles in this book and do very well for yourself. Less is more in finance, so keep it simple—

1. Automatically save 25–50% of your income (before taxes) for your retirement and brokerage accounts.

2. Invest in a low-cost stock index fund until you have at least $250,000, possibly much more if you're saving much more than $25,000 per year.

3. Avoid frequent 20% drawdowns by then investing in a low-cost bond index fund until you retire.

4. Rebalance once per year to 60/40 stocks and bonds when you're near retirement, maybe 30/70 when you're well into retirement.

5. Tune out all the bullshit (everything is bullshit!) and never deviate from this plan.

Your financial destiny and your freedom are ultimately in your hands—no one else will solve your life for you. Everybody wants results, but few want to put in the work to get those results. Don't expect results to fall into your lap, and don't think that paying a financial advisor automatically gets you results either.

Once you've learned the Basic and Intermediate Plans and can implement them with minimal effort, you'll give yourself the gift of time. This time will allow you to focus on other important aspects of your life—career, family, relationships, fun hobbies, personal growth, giving back to the world—and you'll never have to worry about money again.

If you're still struggling after reading this book, email me directly at drew@financebro.net. I'm more than happy to help anyone invest their money.

ABOUT THE AUTHOR

DREW WYNN is an investment professional who trades in global macro markets—bonds, credit, currencies, commodities, and equity indexes. He oversees millions of dollars and has helped friends and family decisively outperform the market since 2014. He was a professional poker player from 2010–2013 and a sales trader at a big oil company for several years before that.

He received a bachelor's degree in finance and international business from the Kelley School of Business at Indiana University in 2007. He currently lives in Asheville, North Carolina and performs improv comedy around town.

Find out more about Drew at FinanceBro.net.

www.ingramcontent.com/pod-product-compliance
Lightning Source LLC
Chambersburg PA
CBHW071409210526
45465CB00001B/311